This Book Belongs

To..........................

....

COLOR TEST PAGE

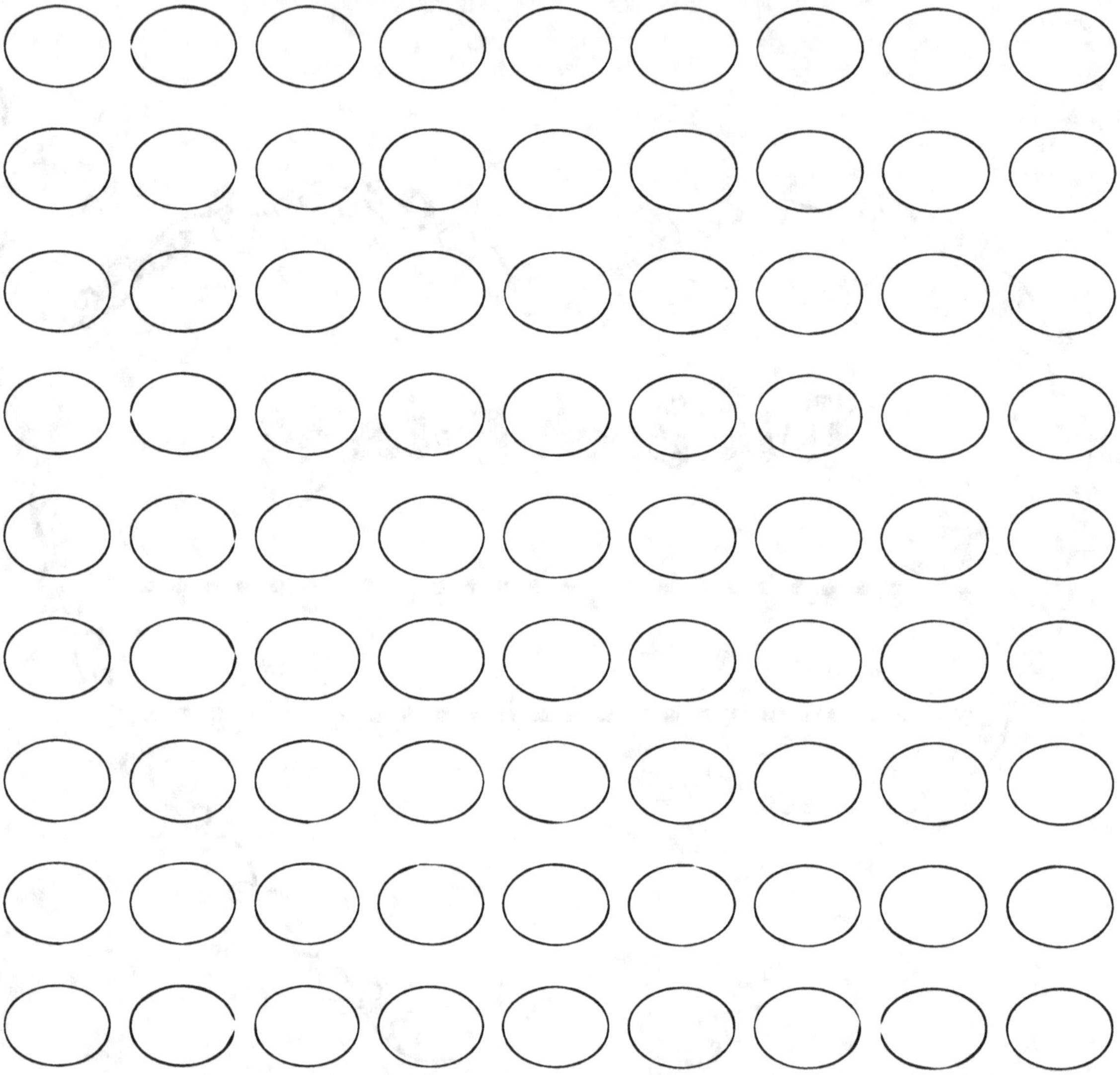

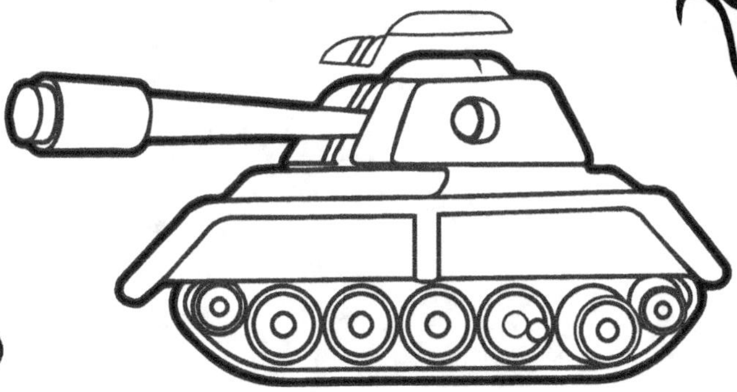

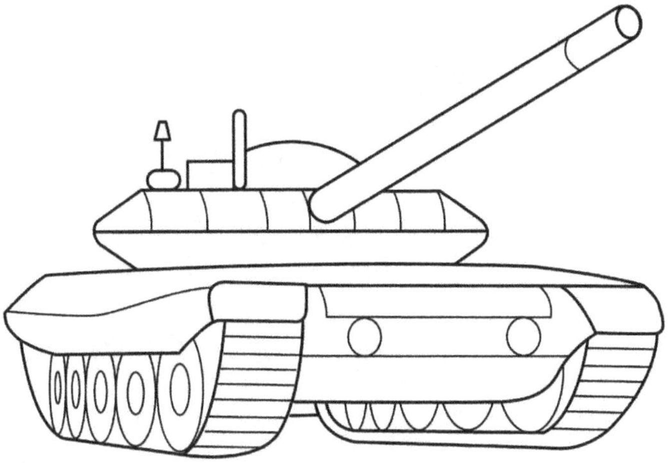

Tank Coloring Book

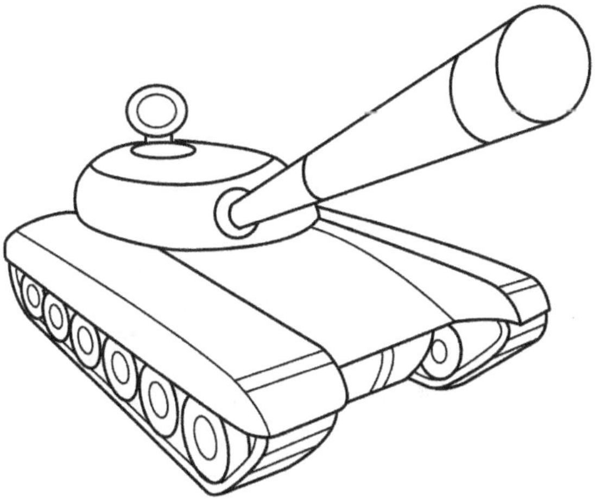

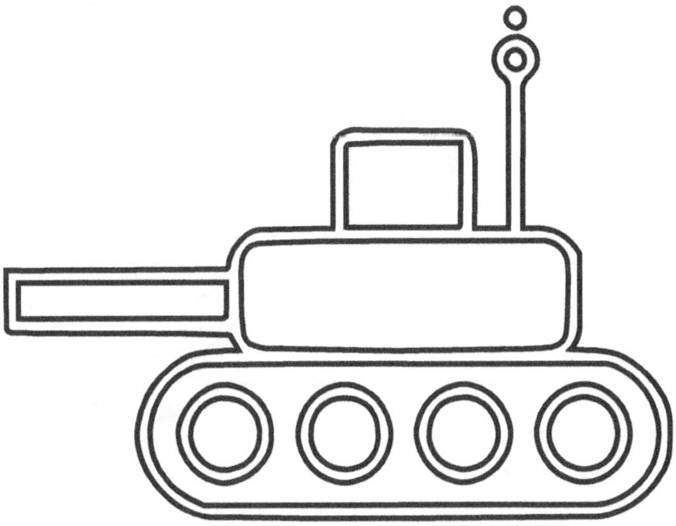

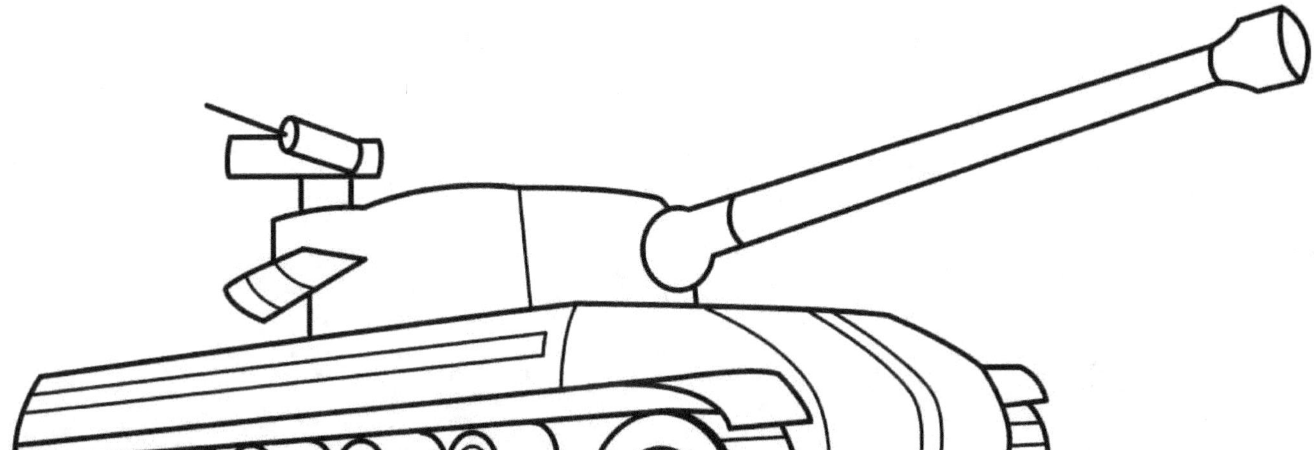

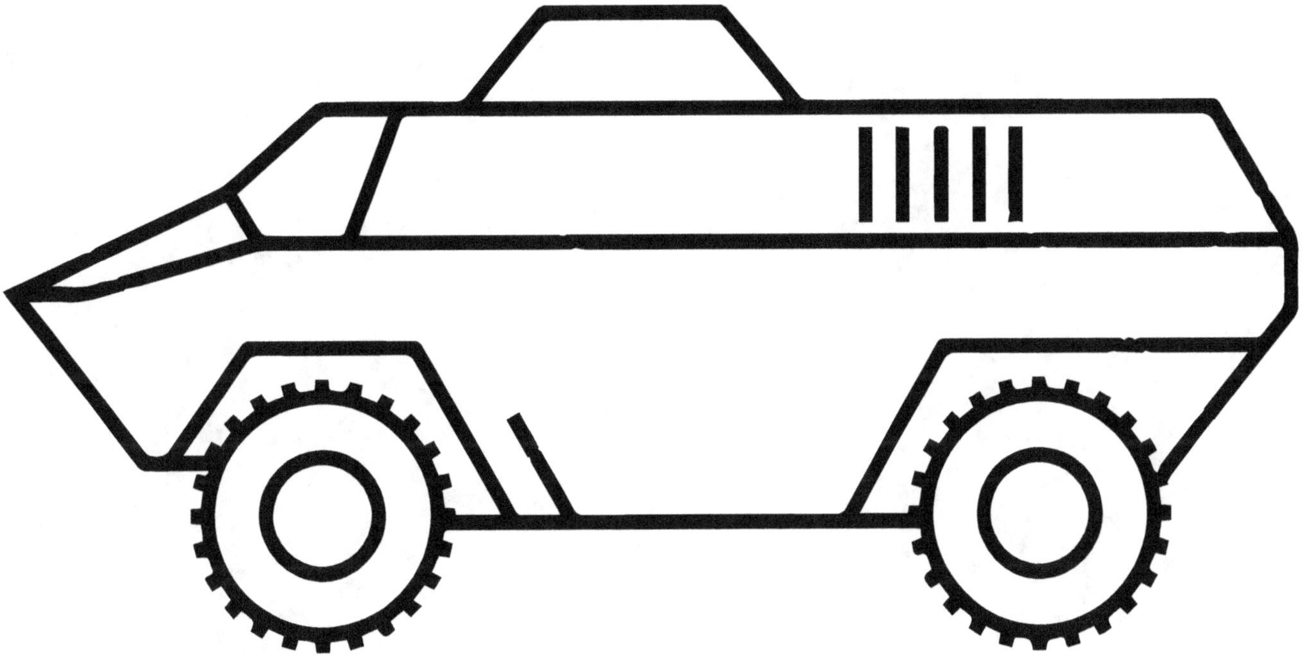

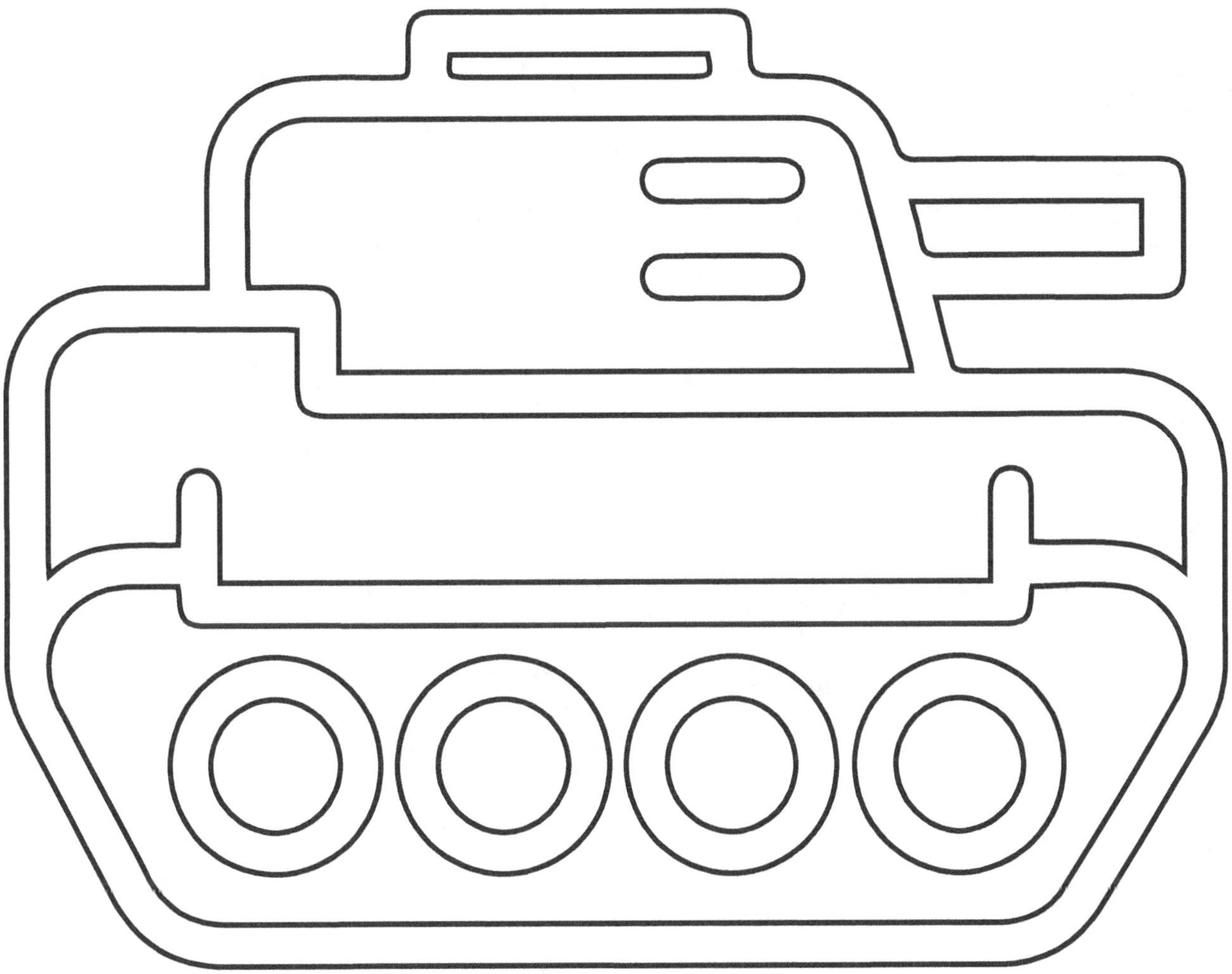

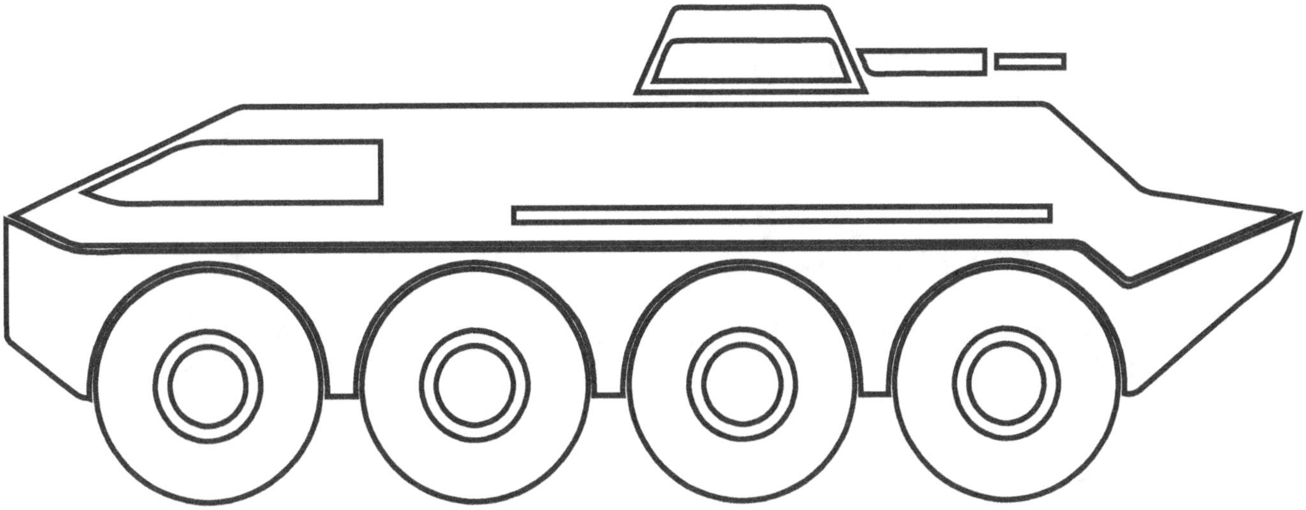

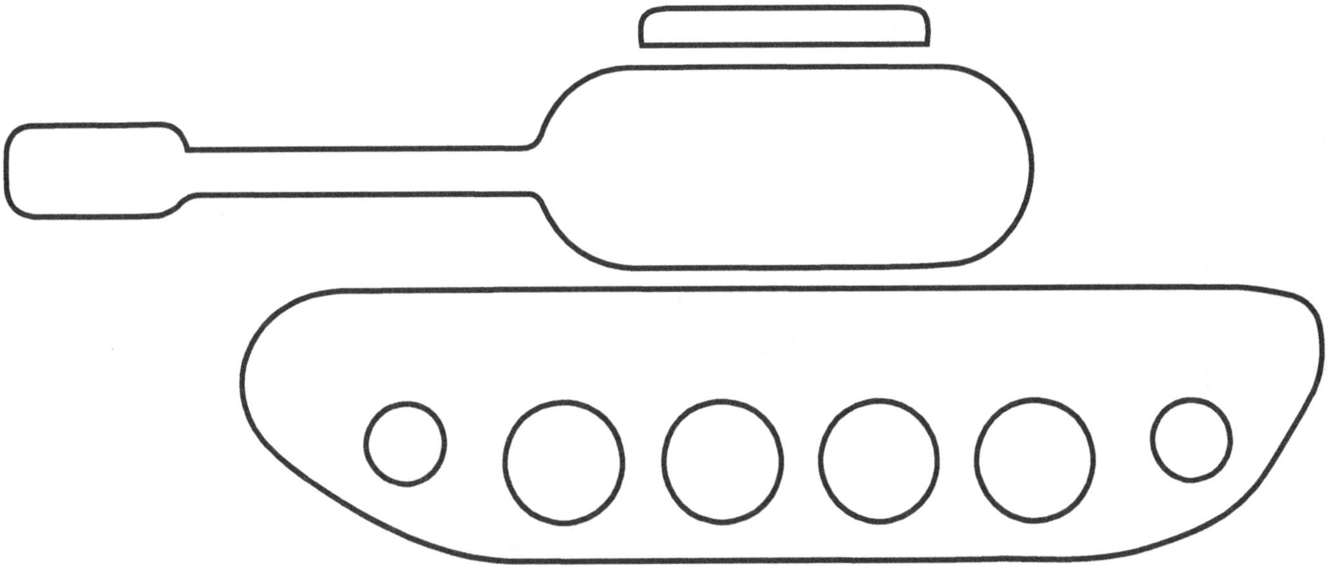

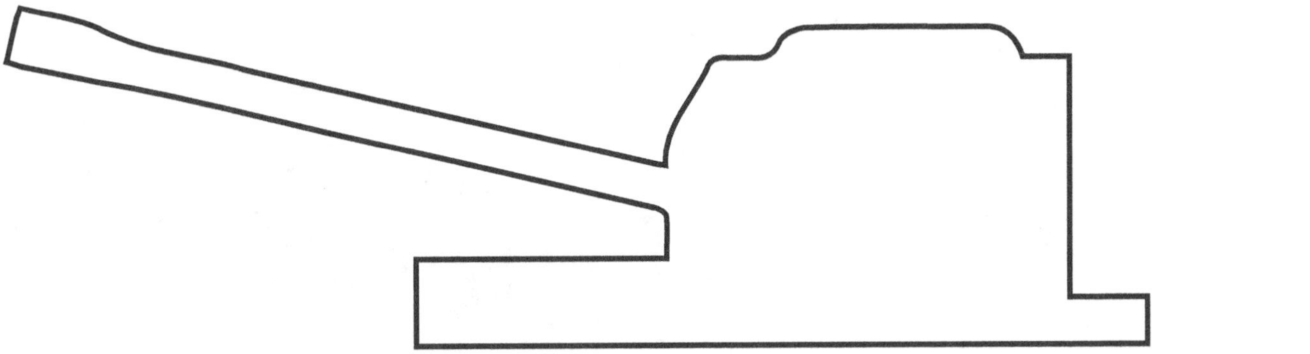

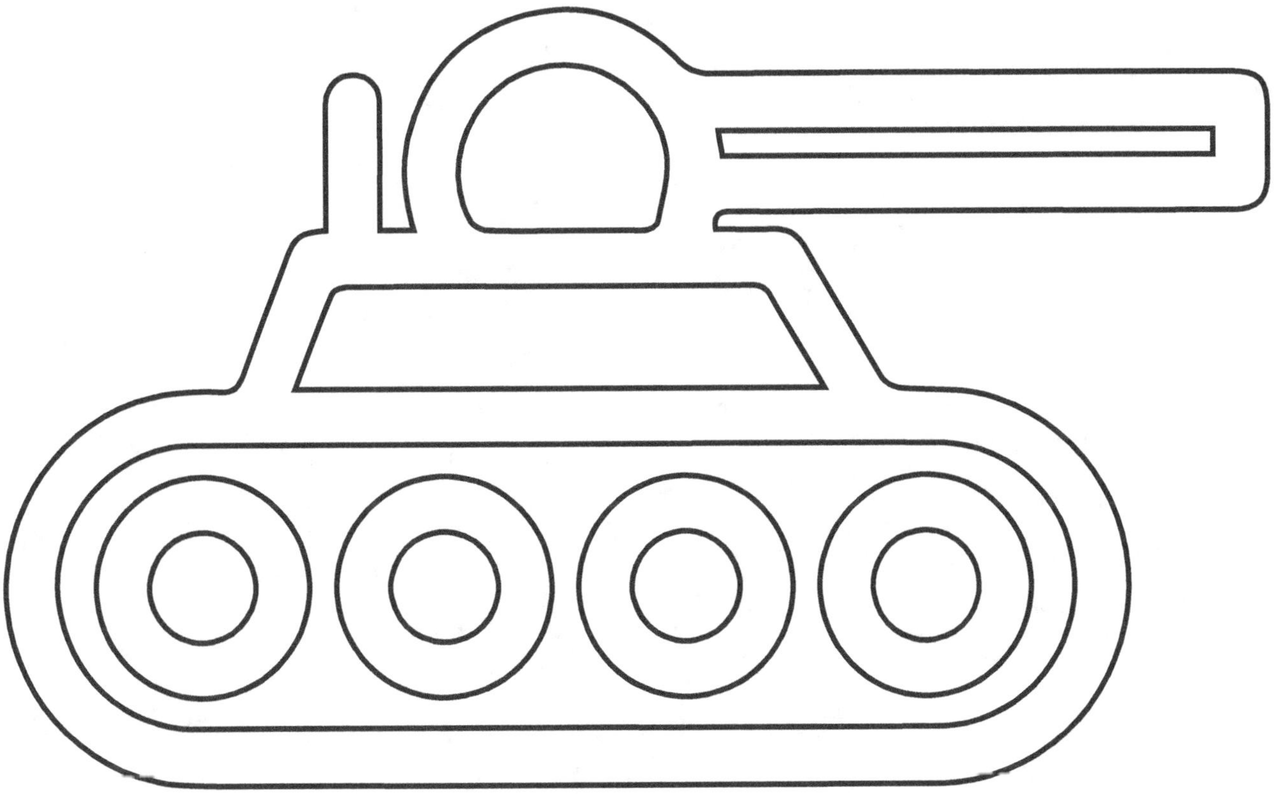

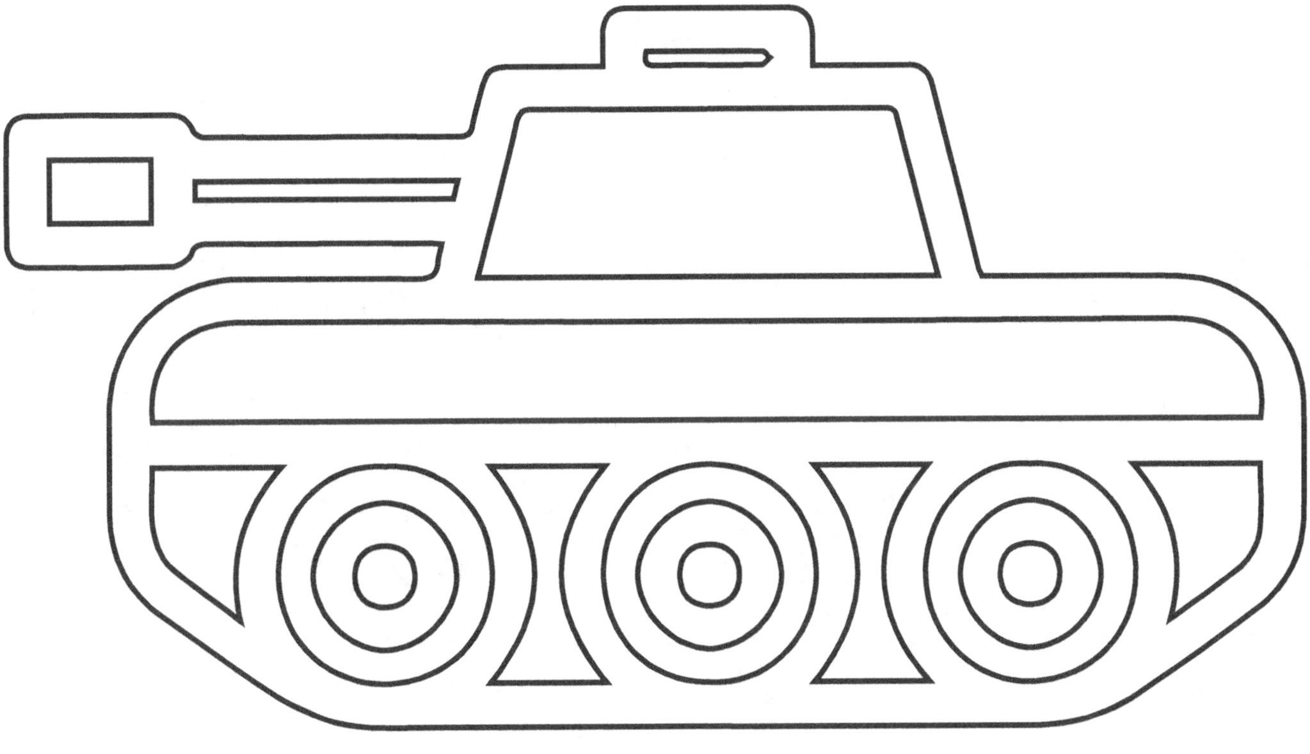

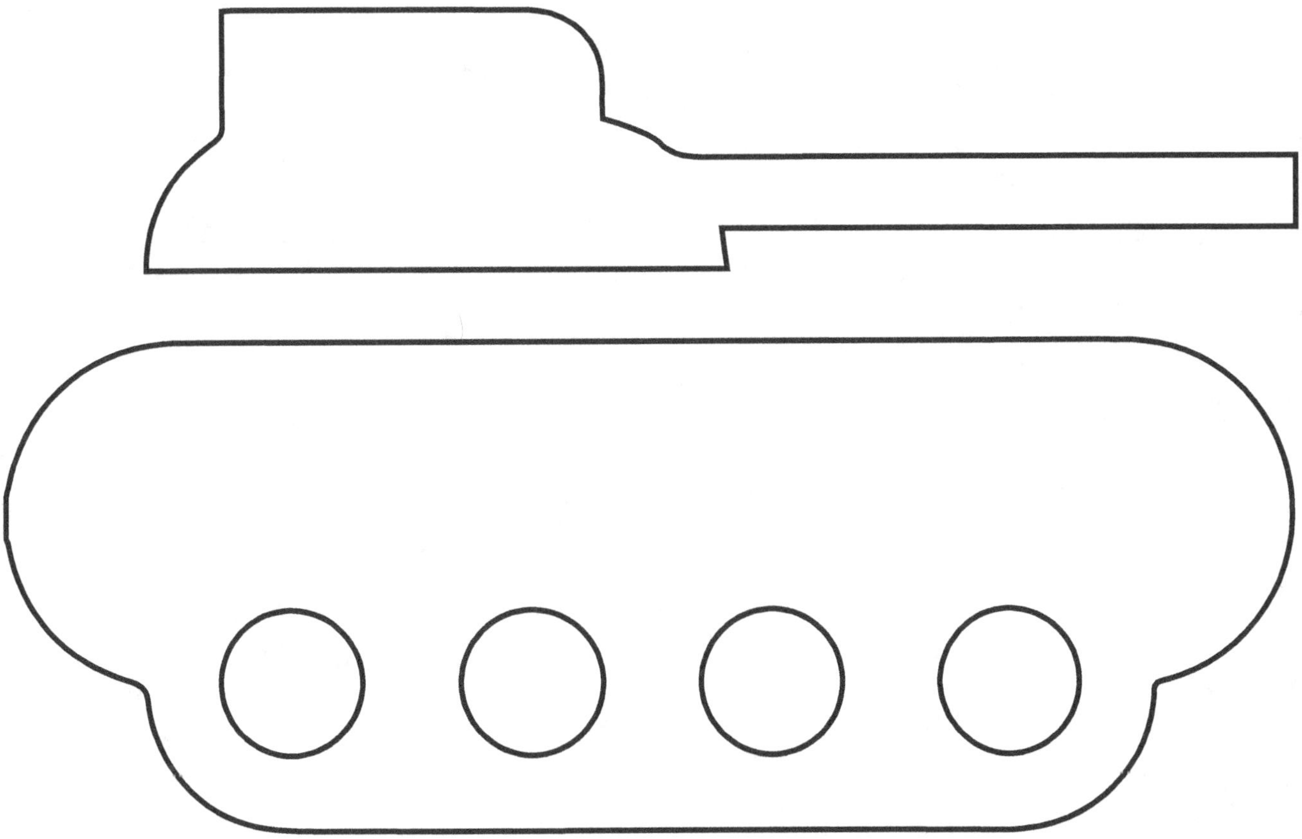

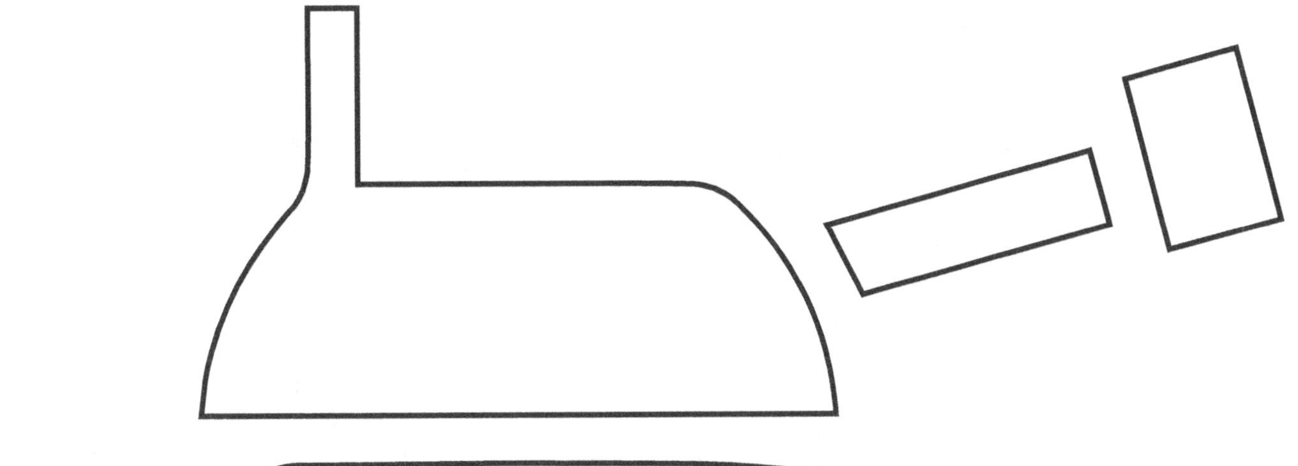

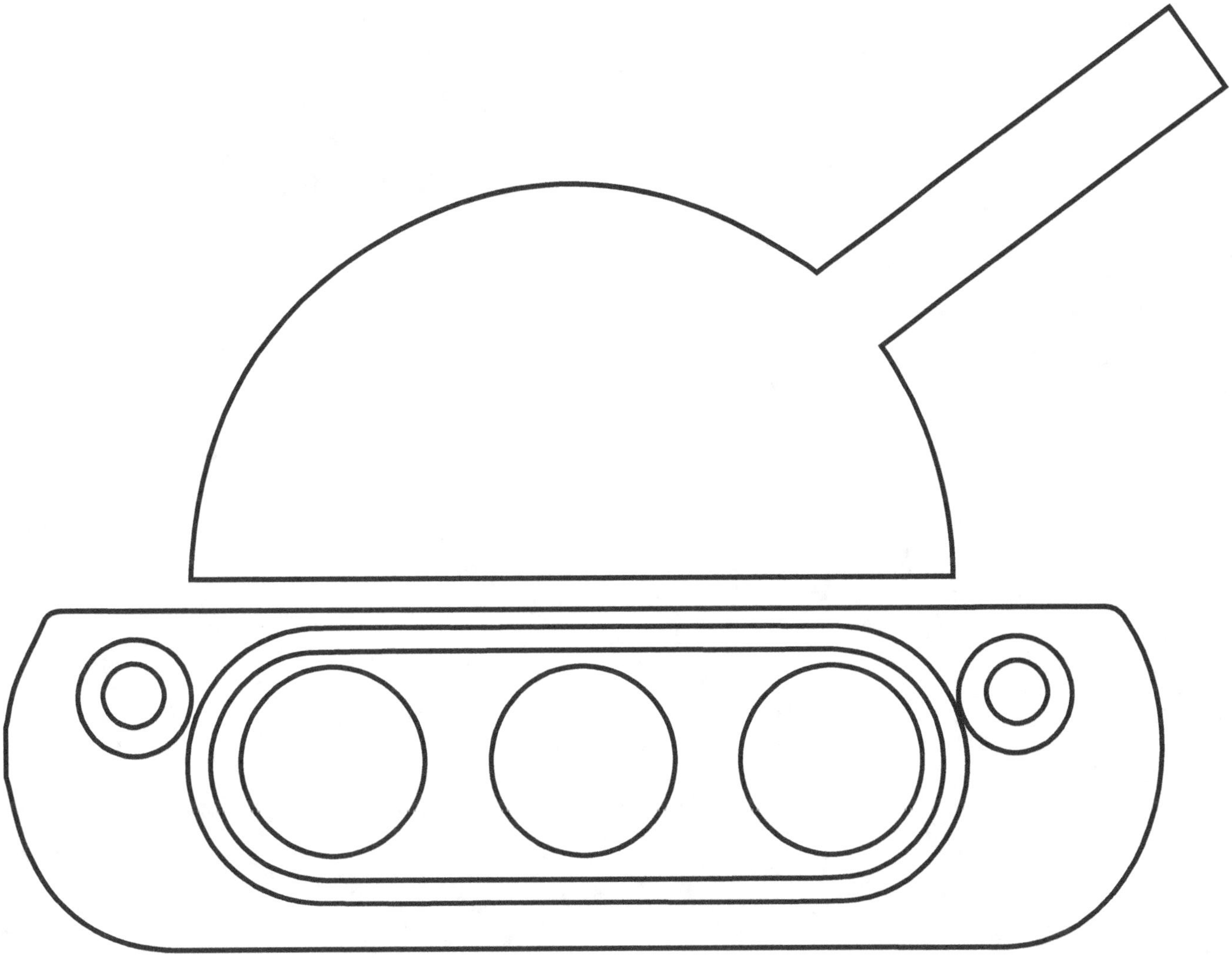

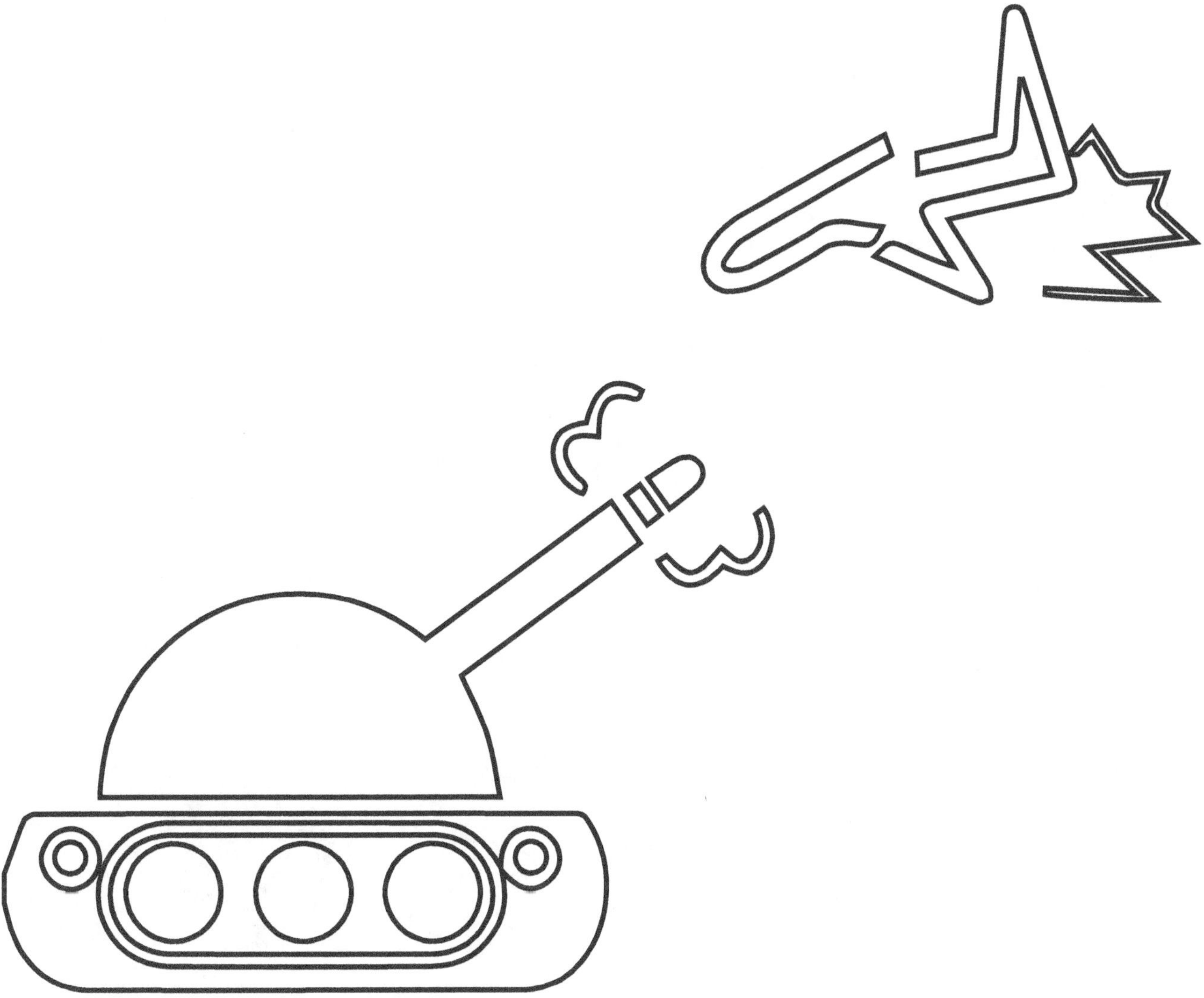

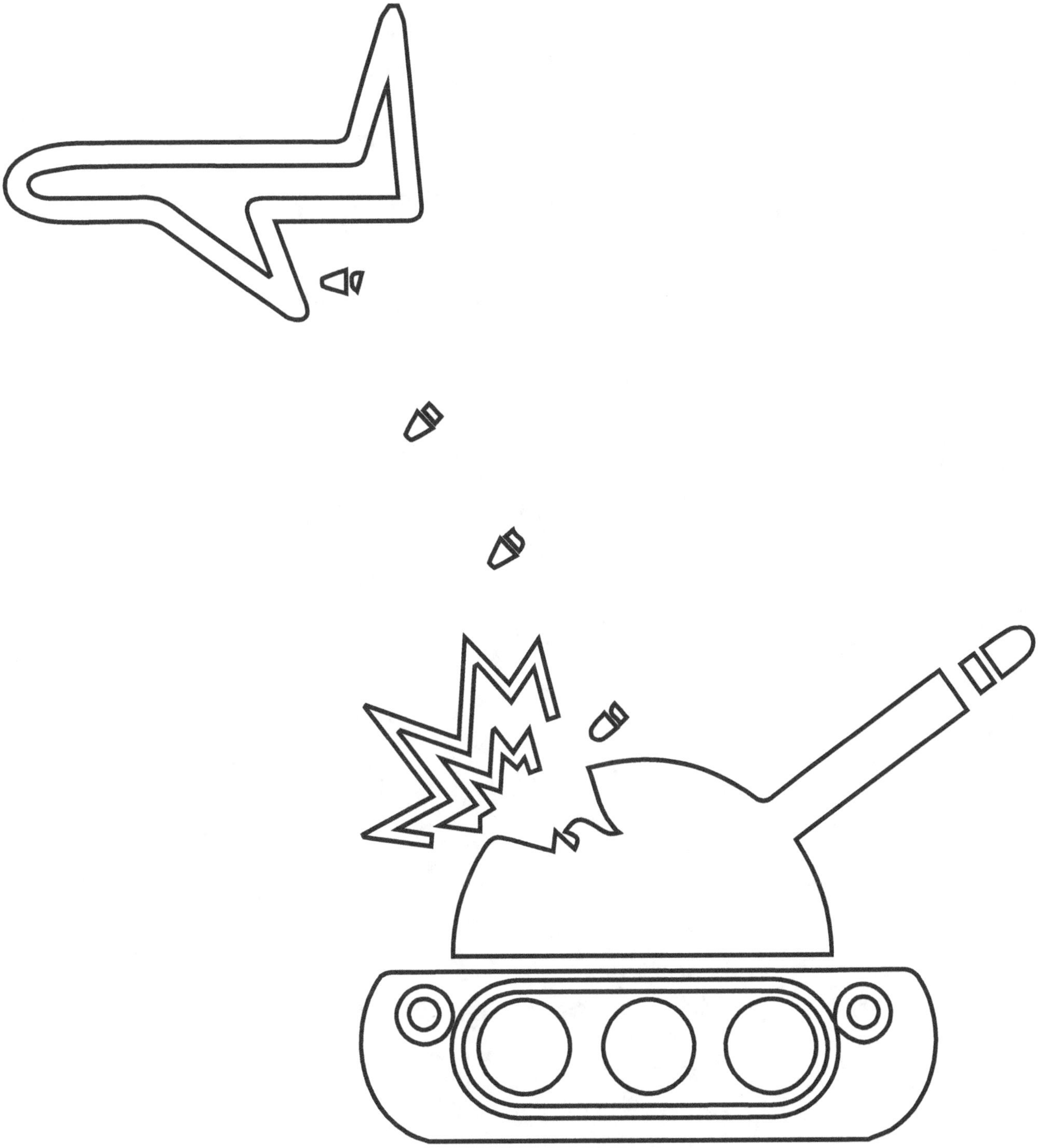

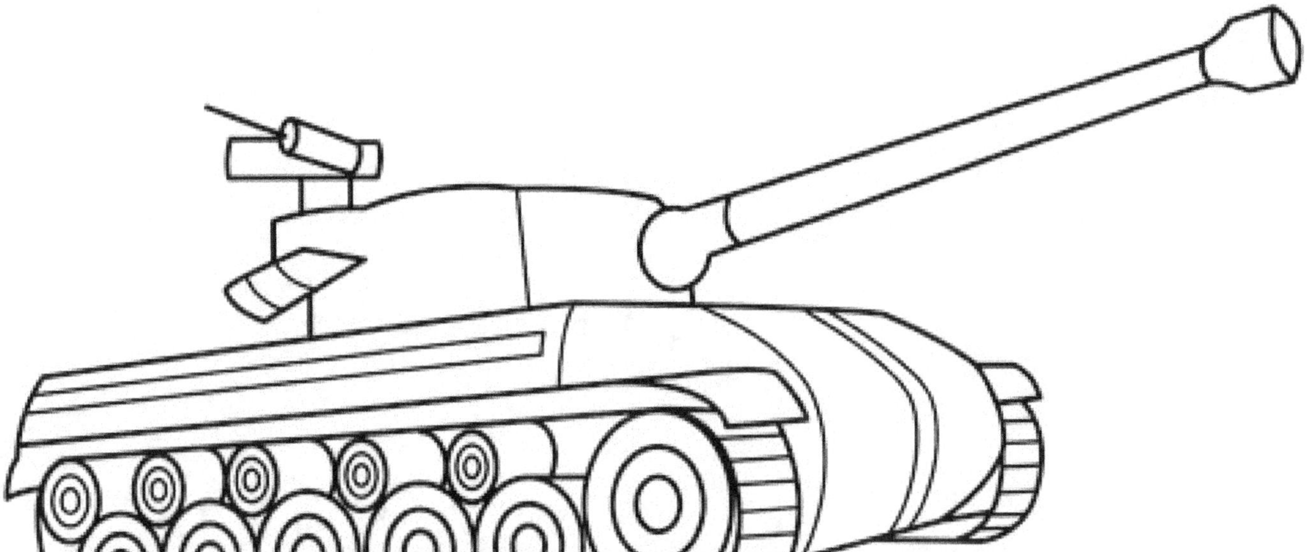

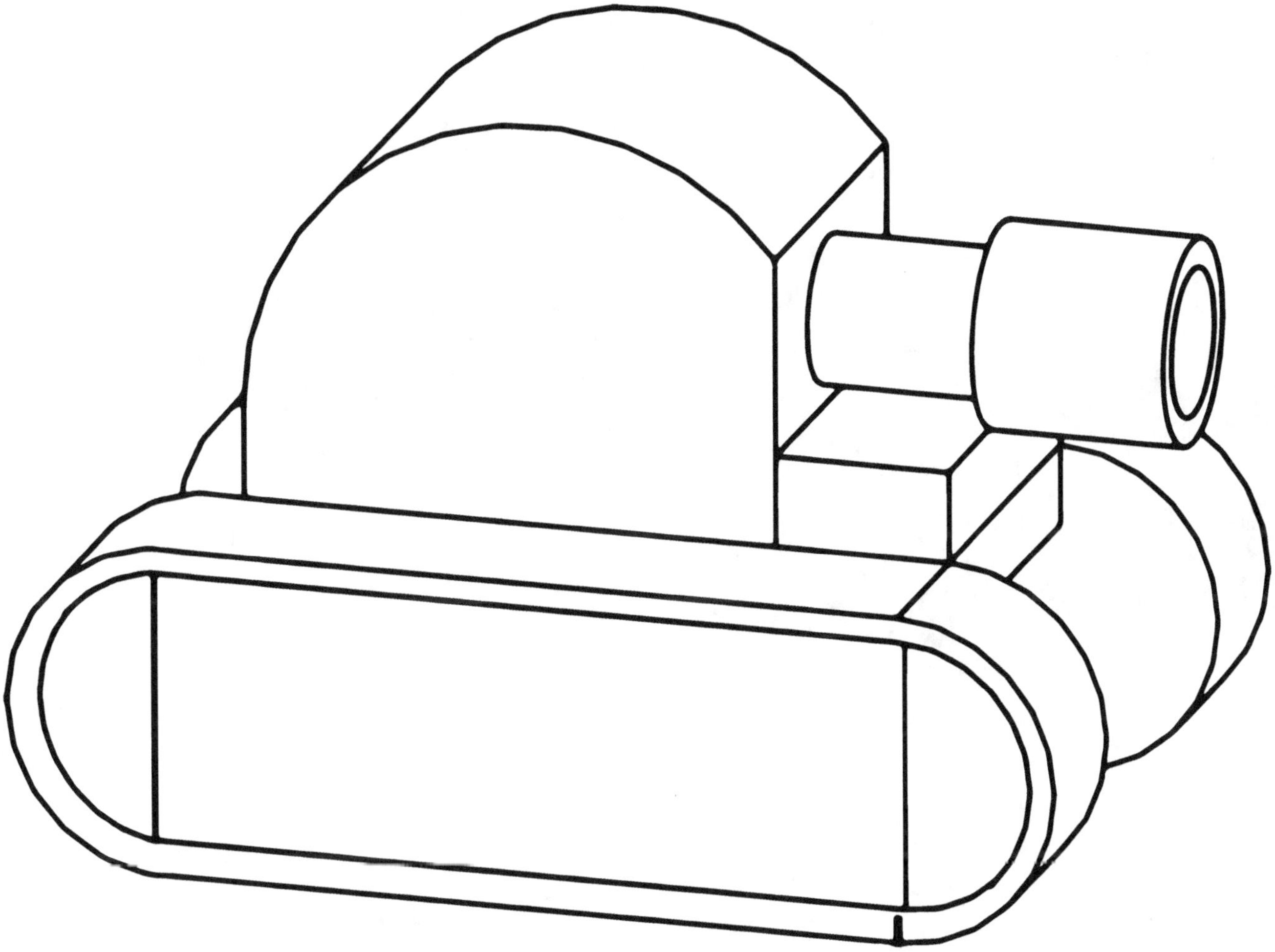

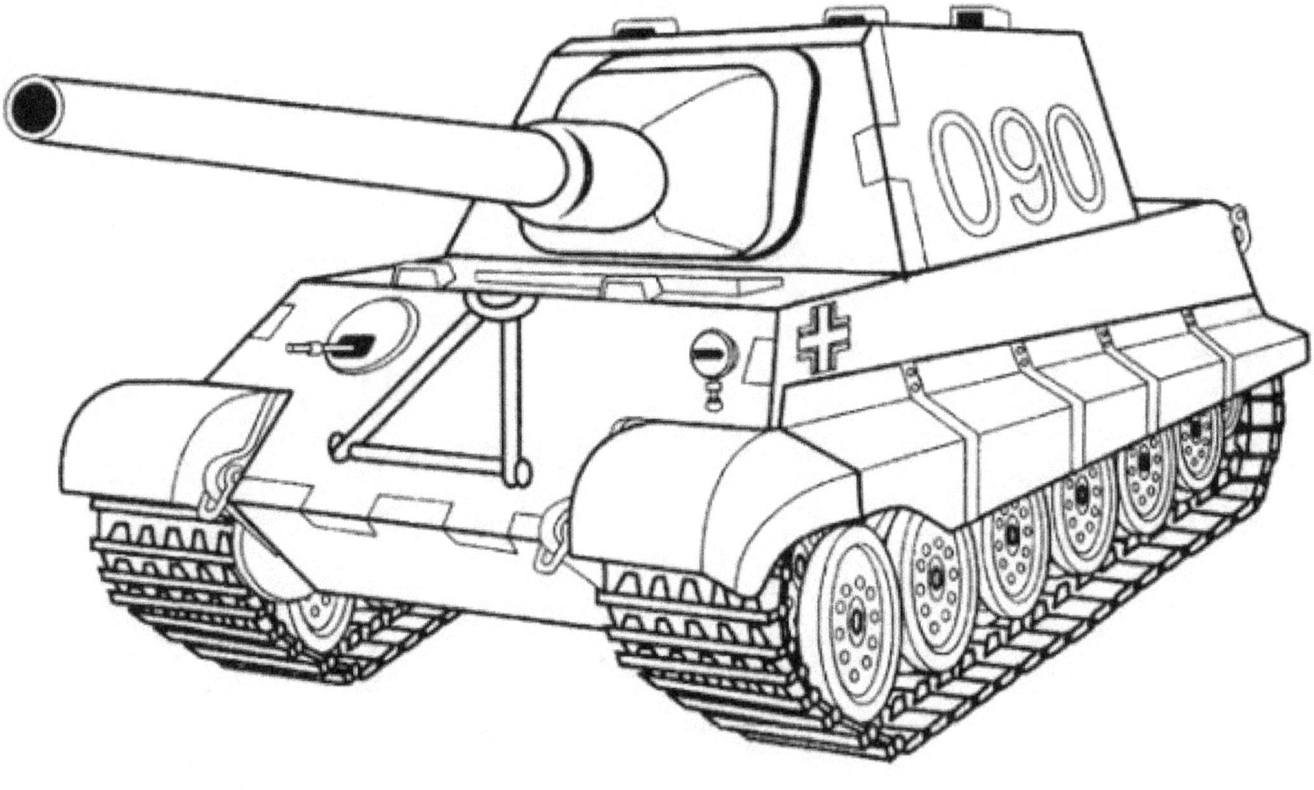
090

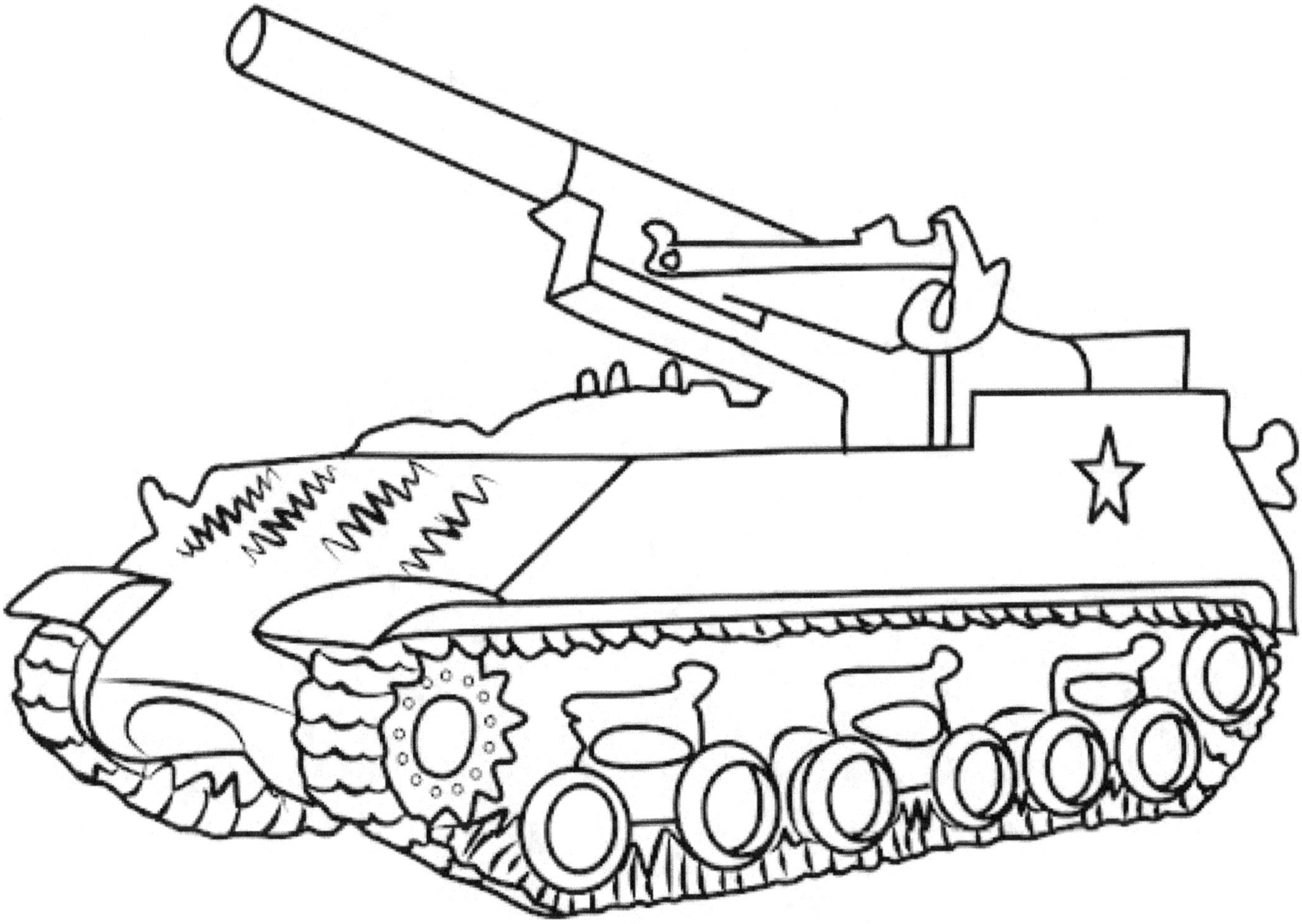

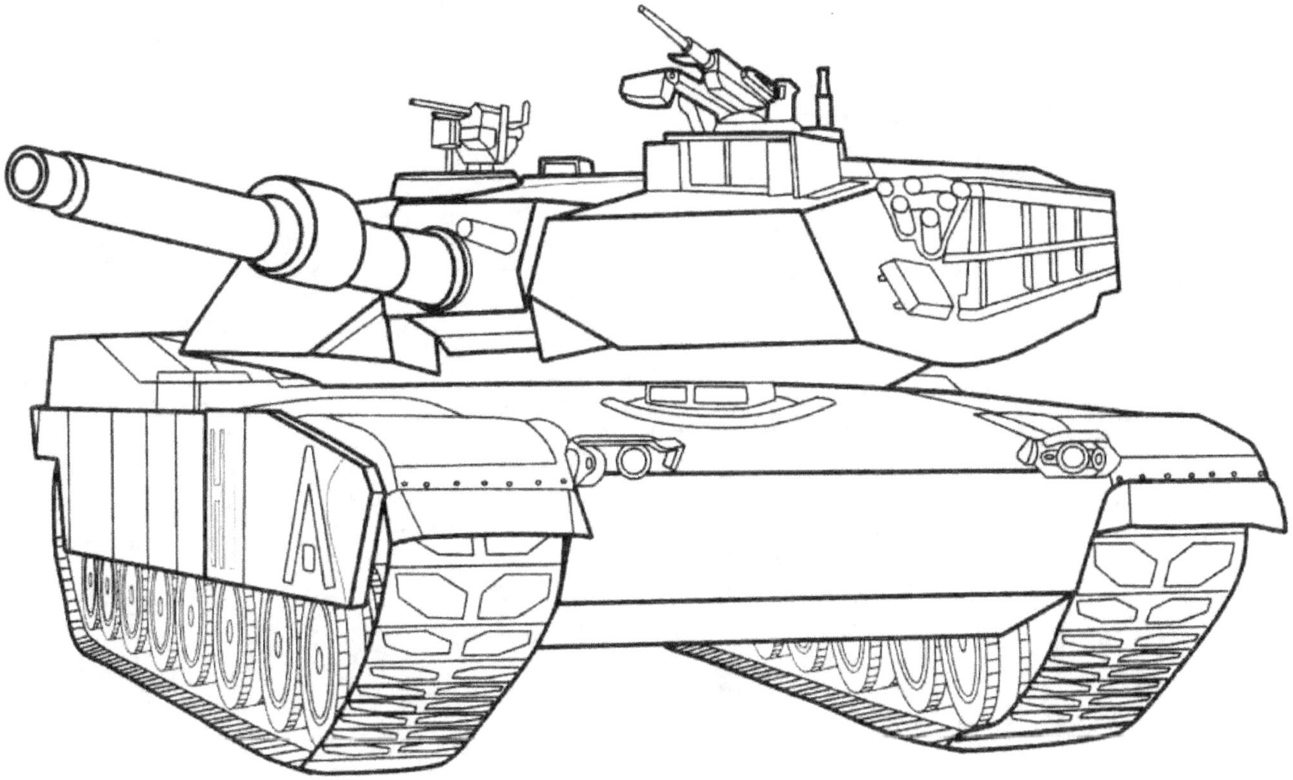

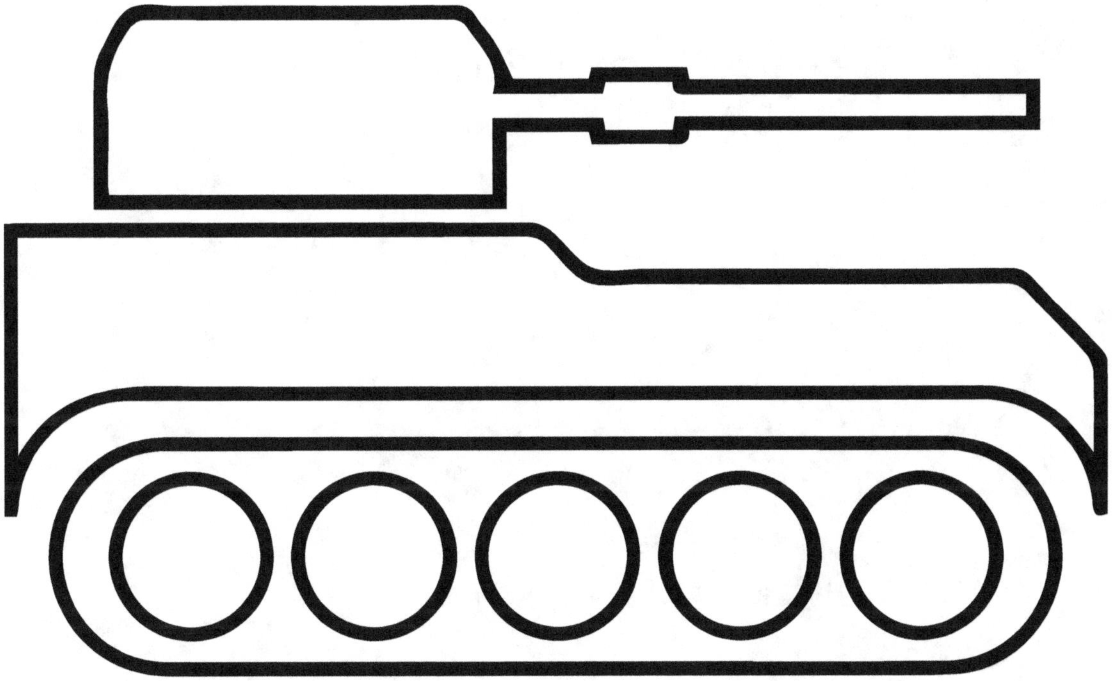

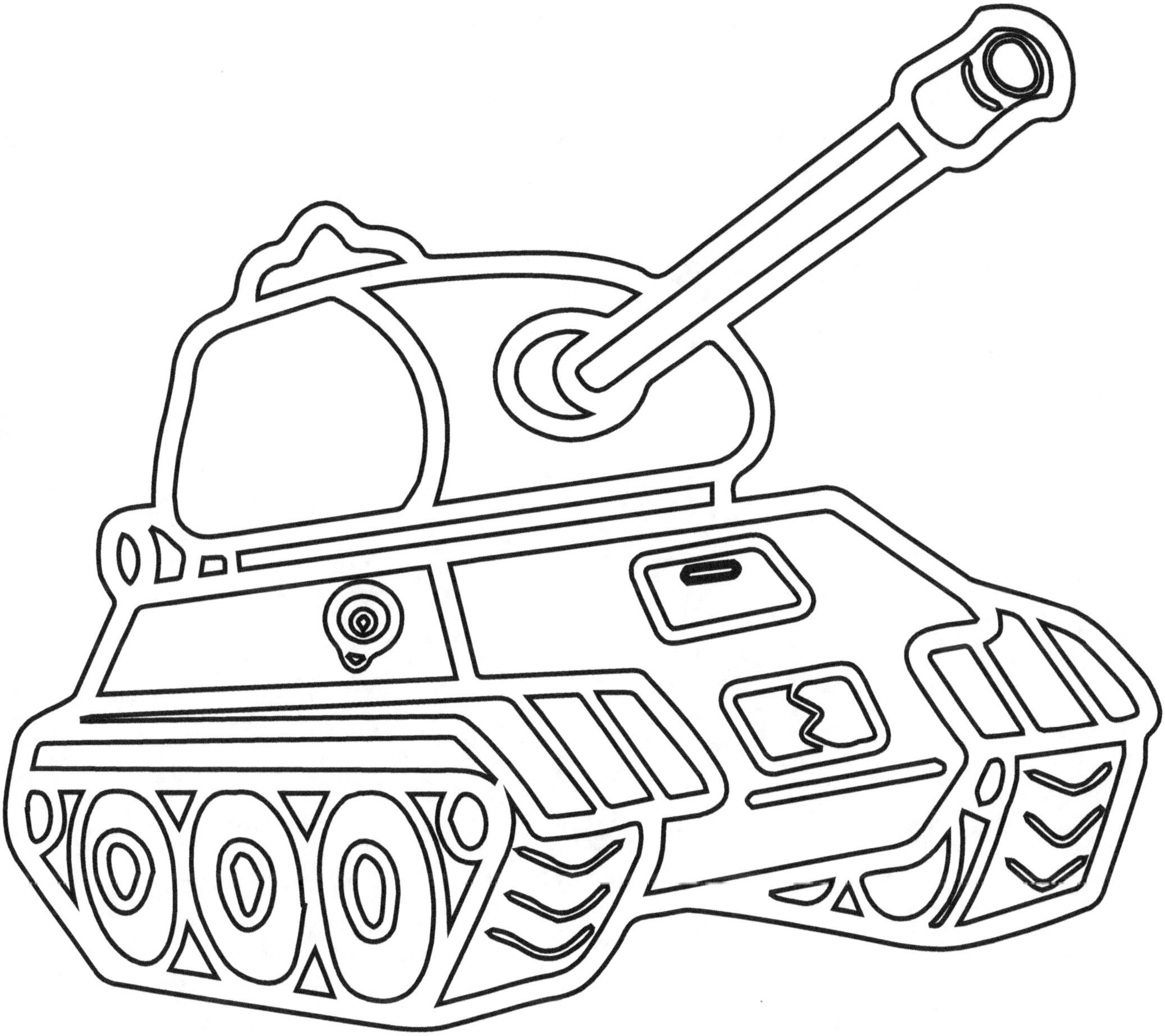

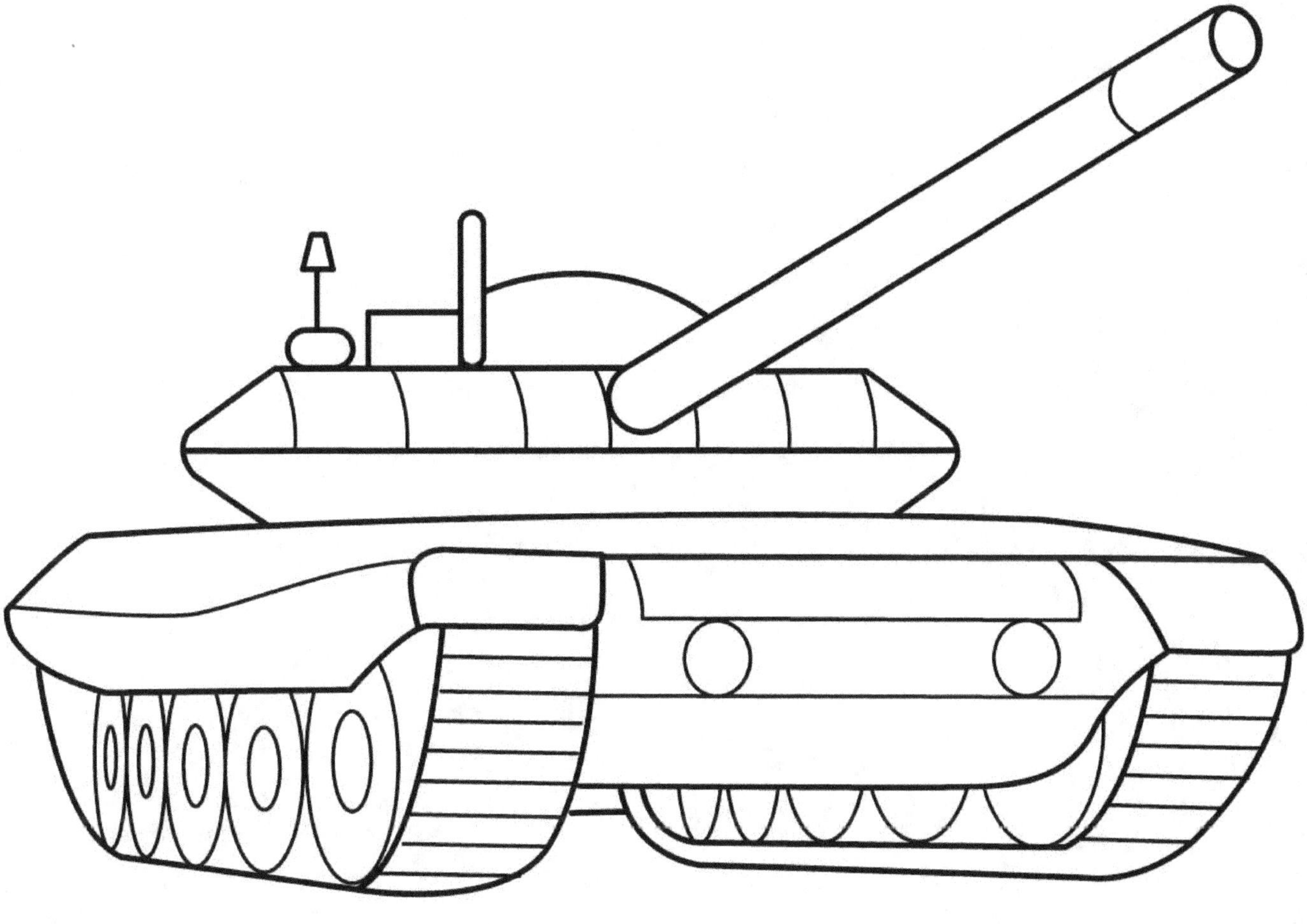

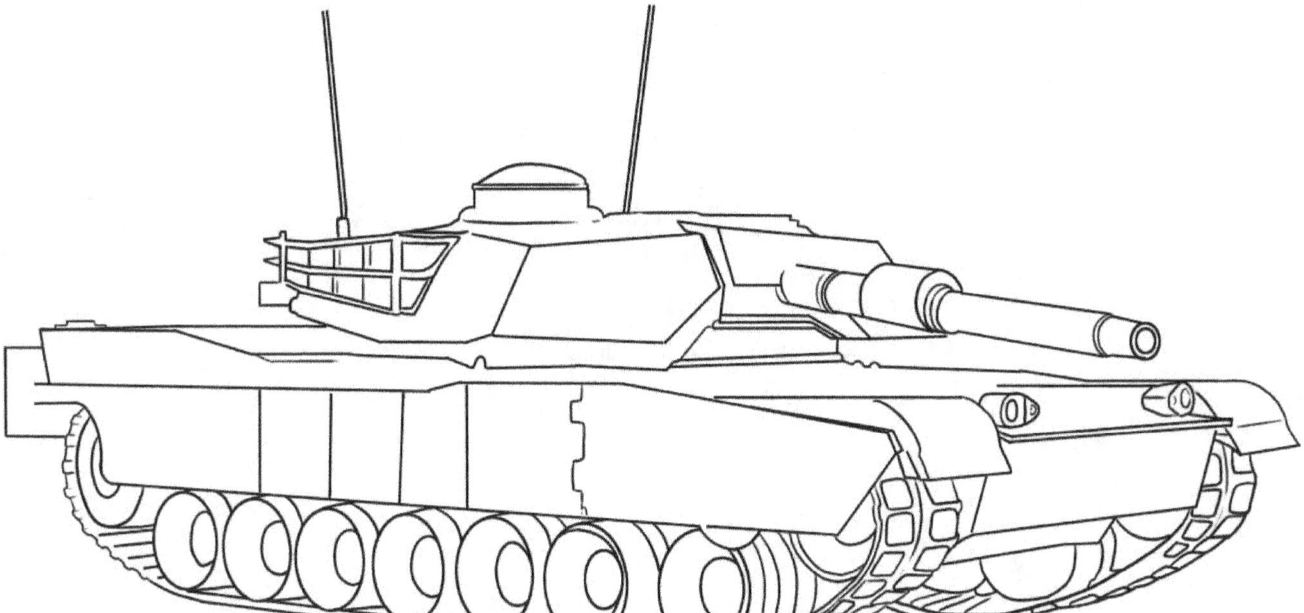

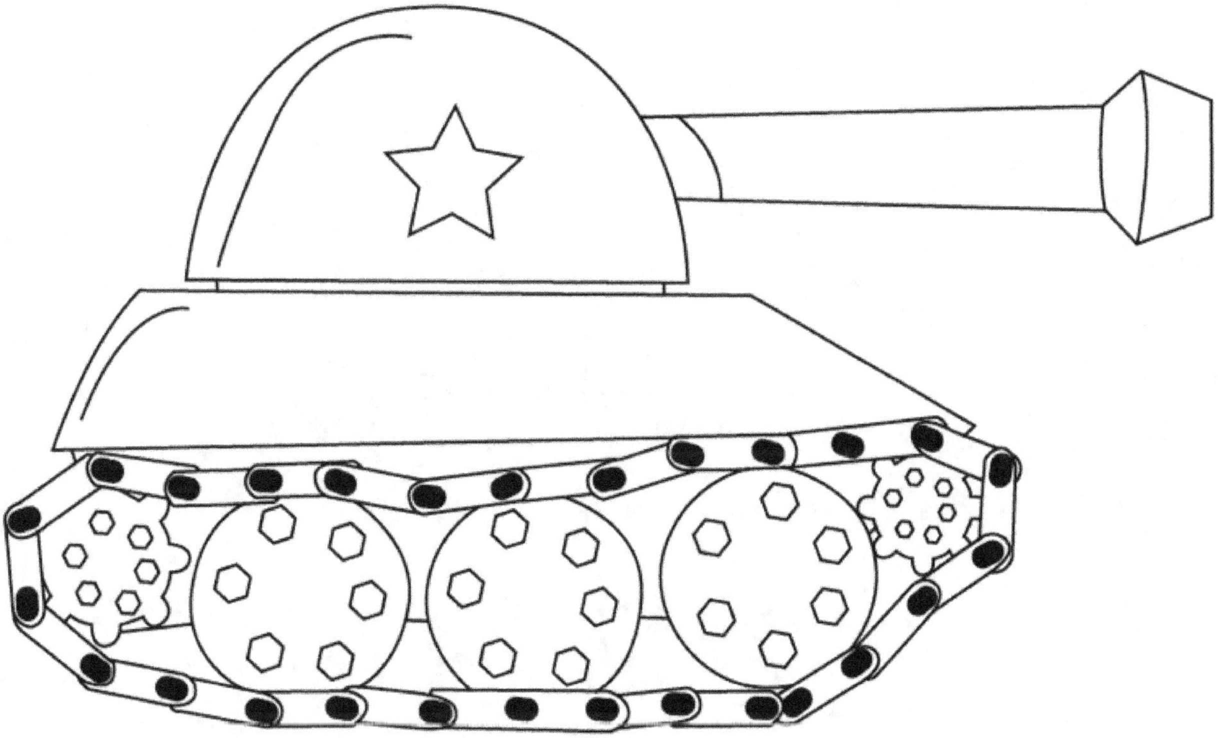

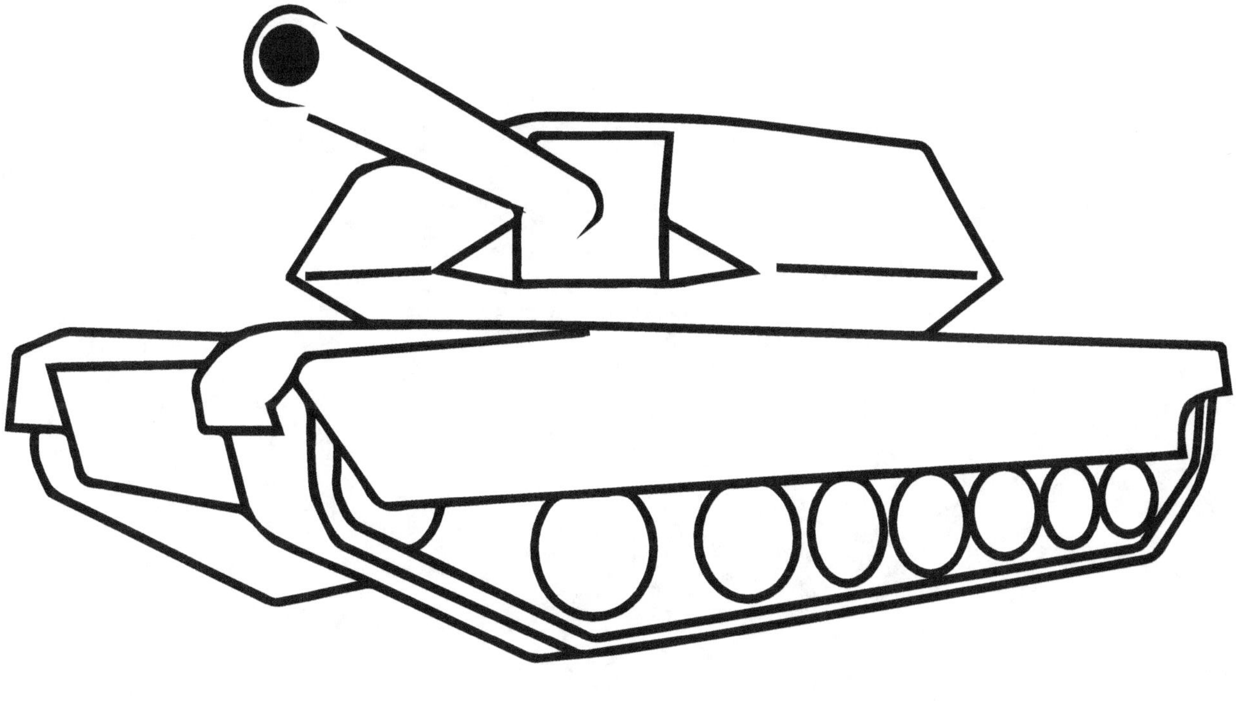

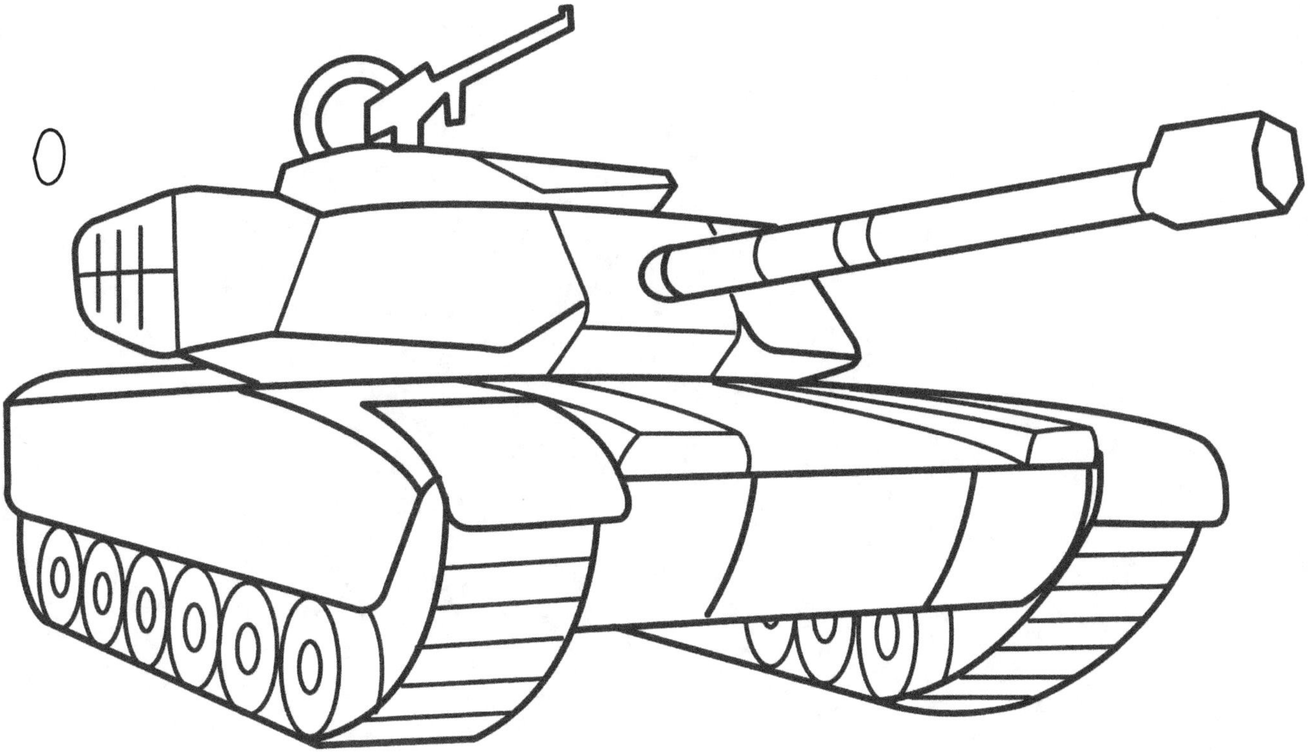

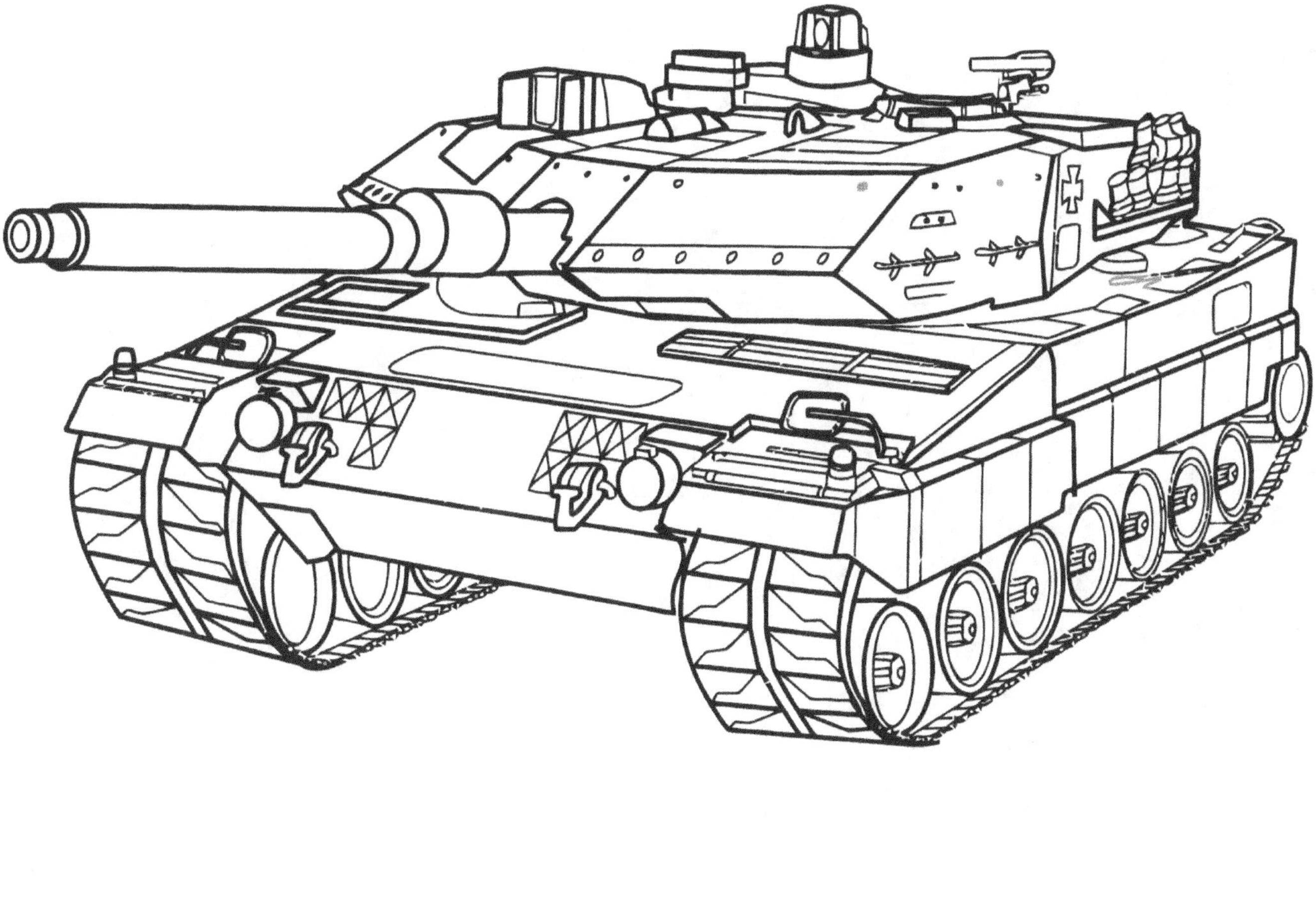

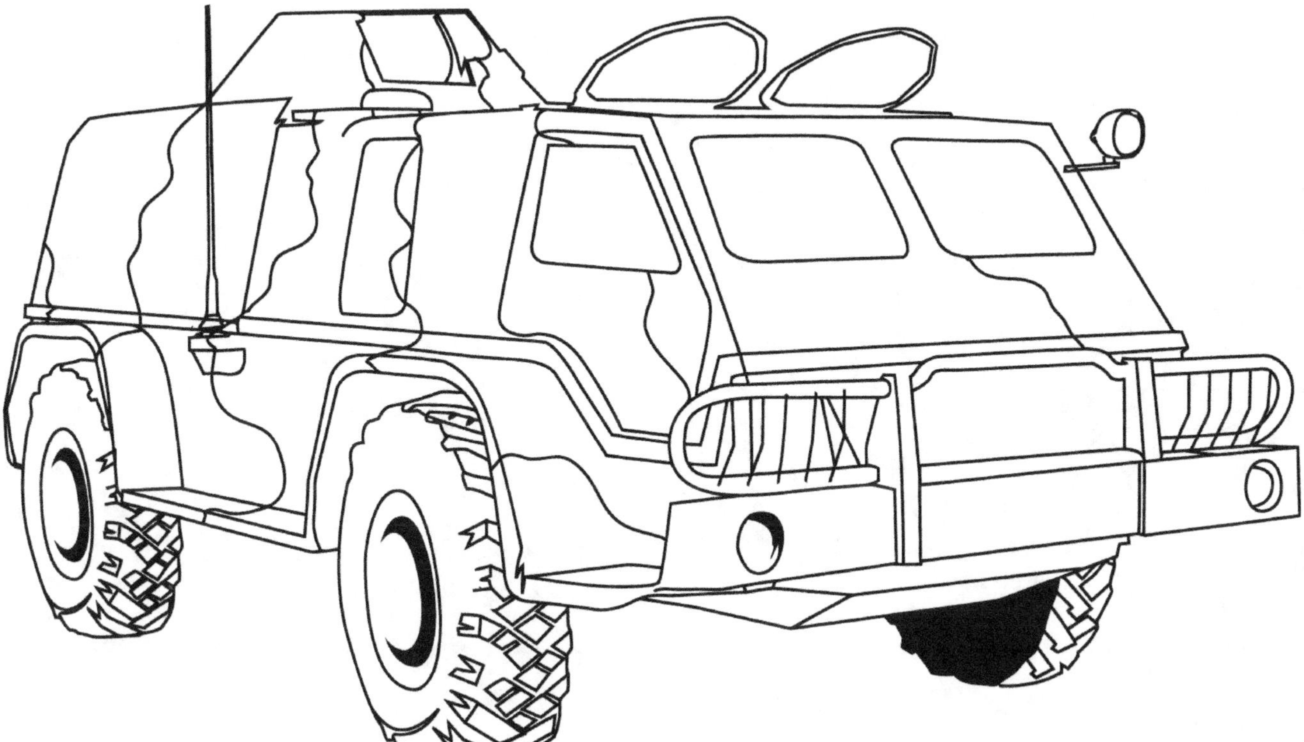

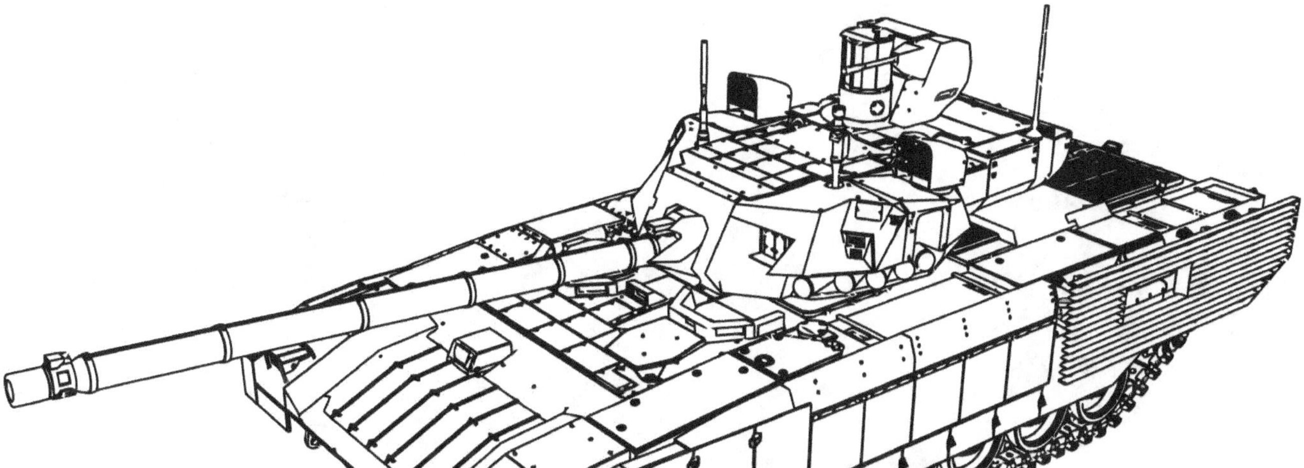

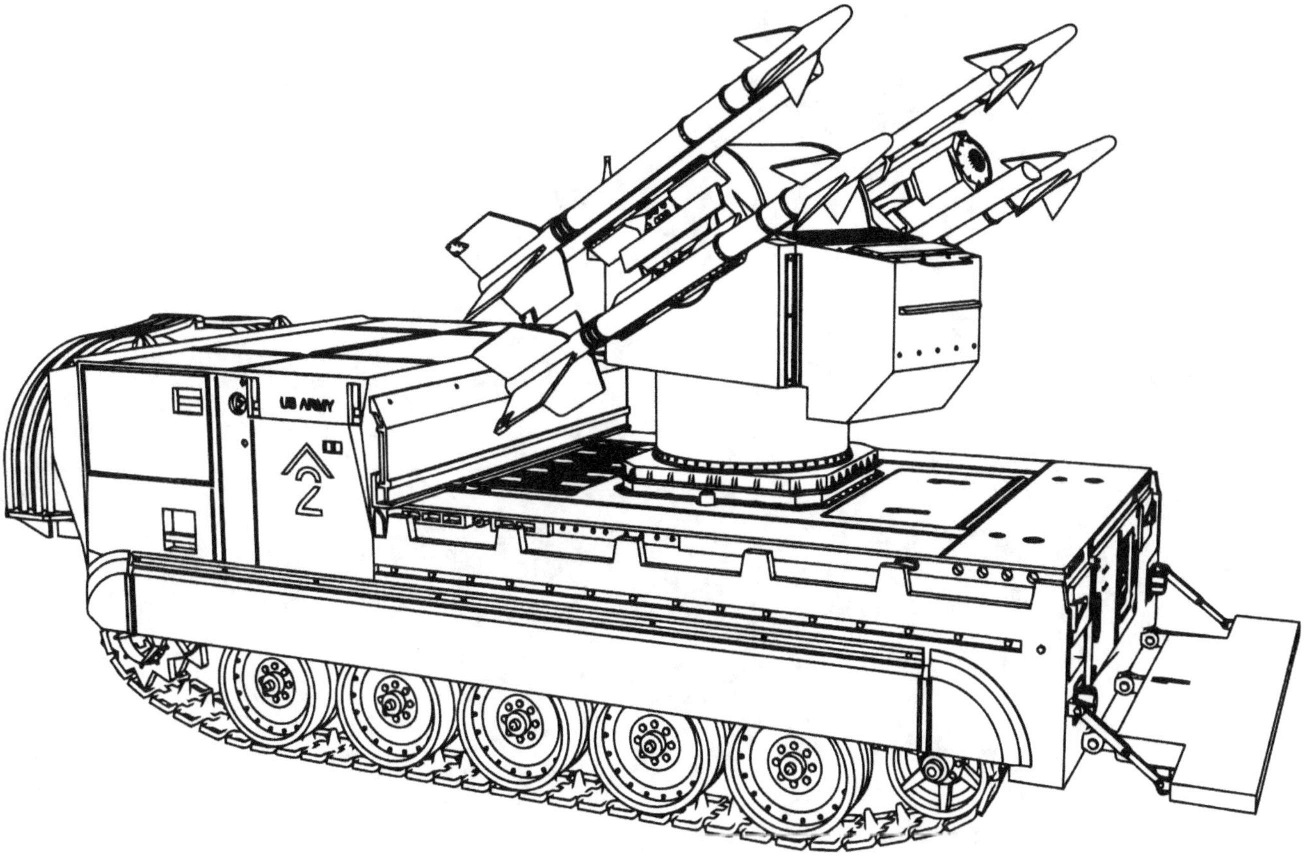
US ARMY

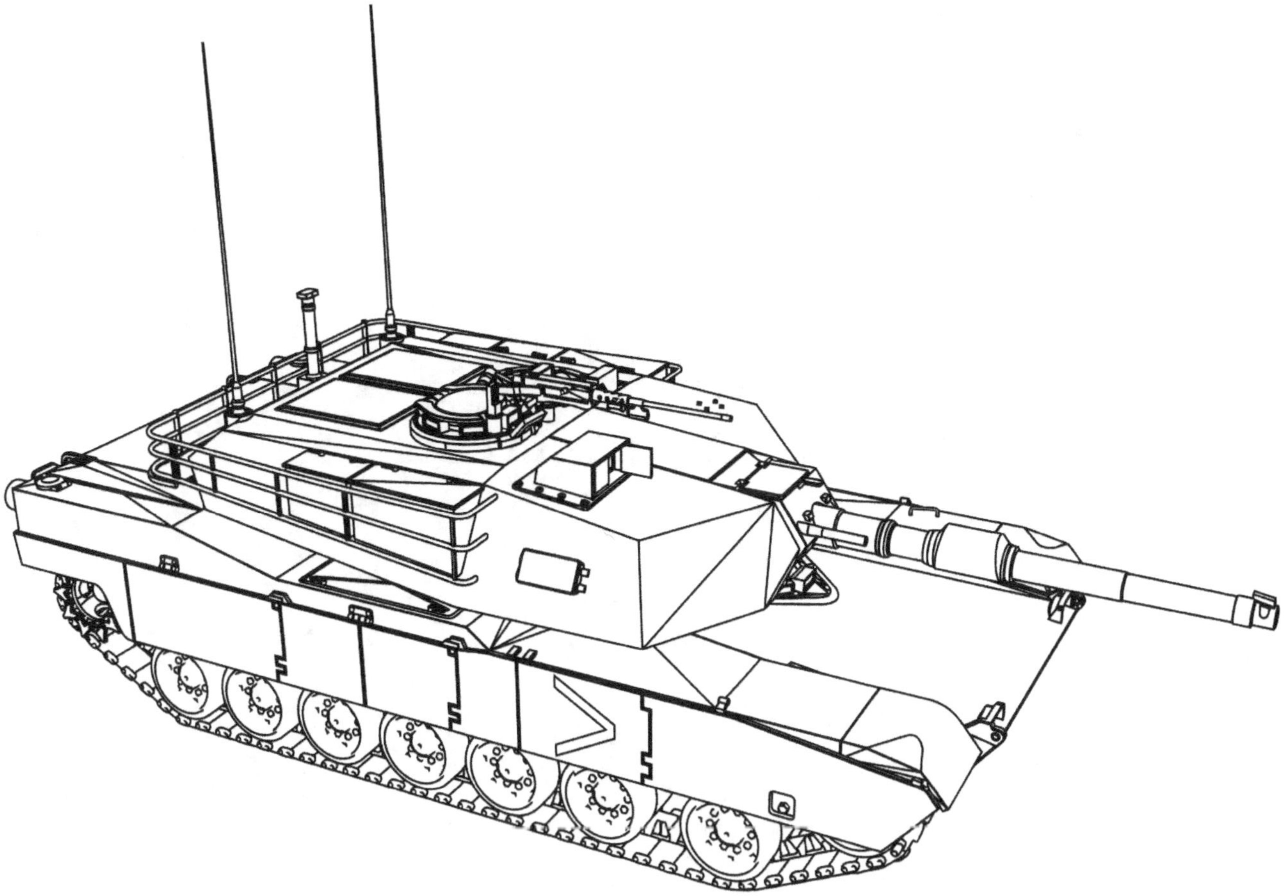

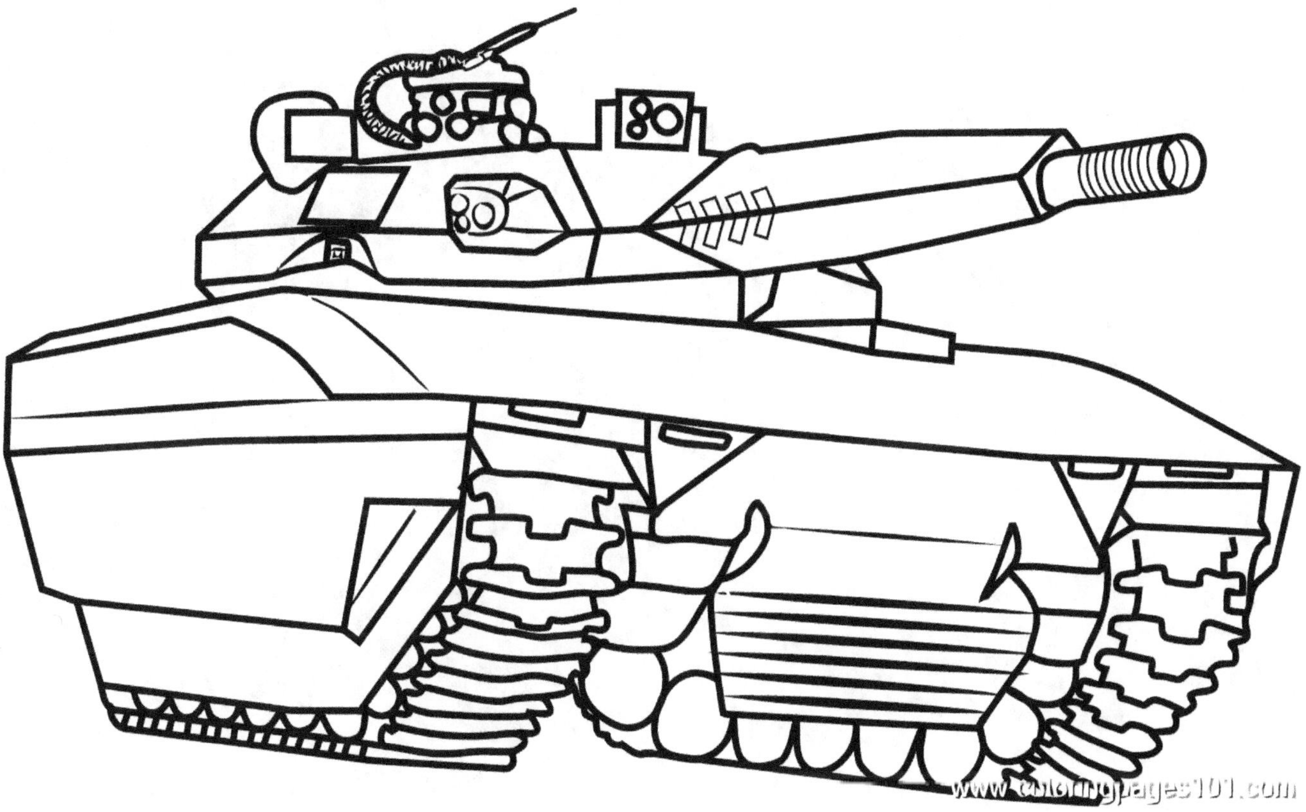
80
80

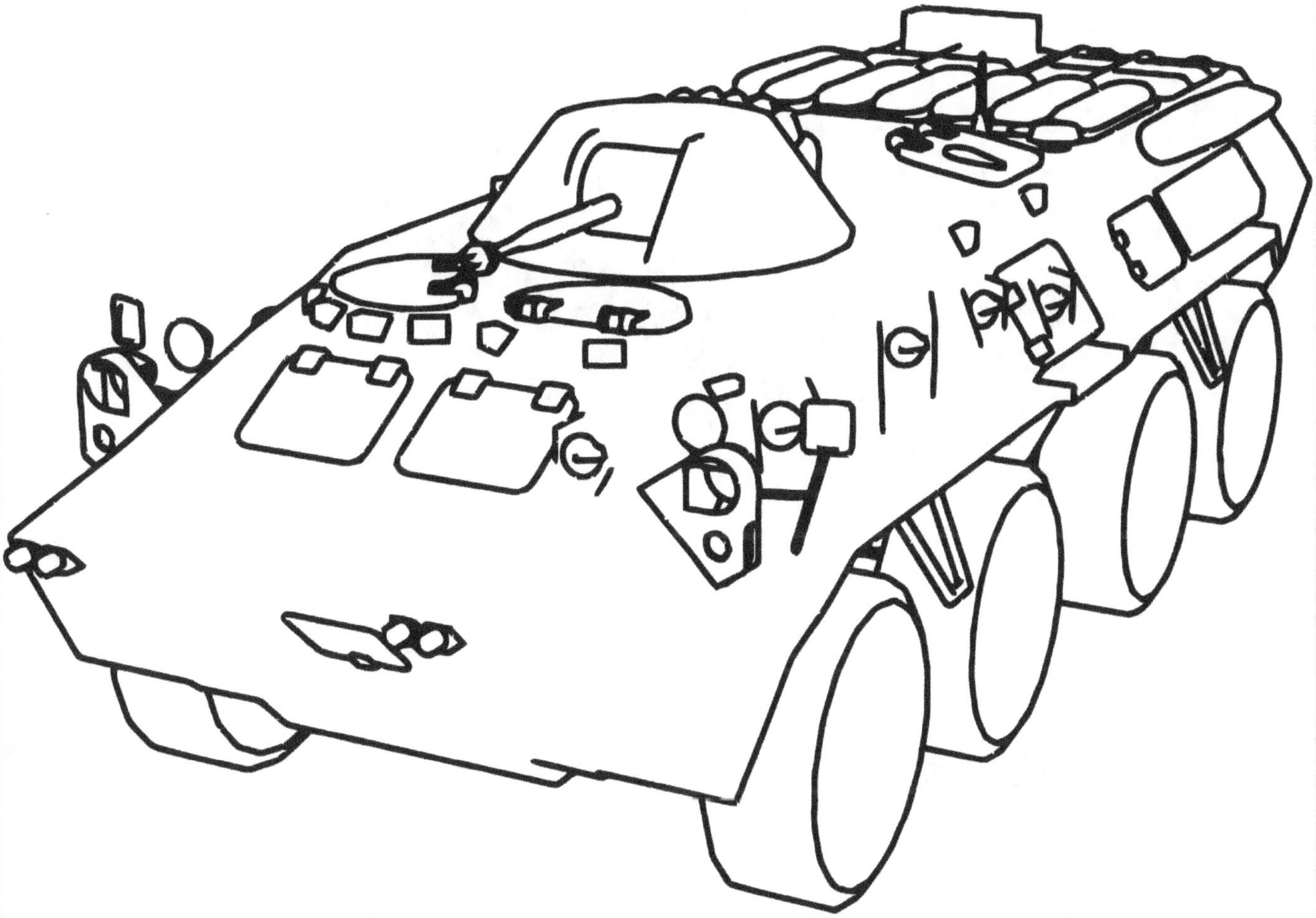

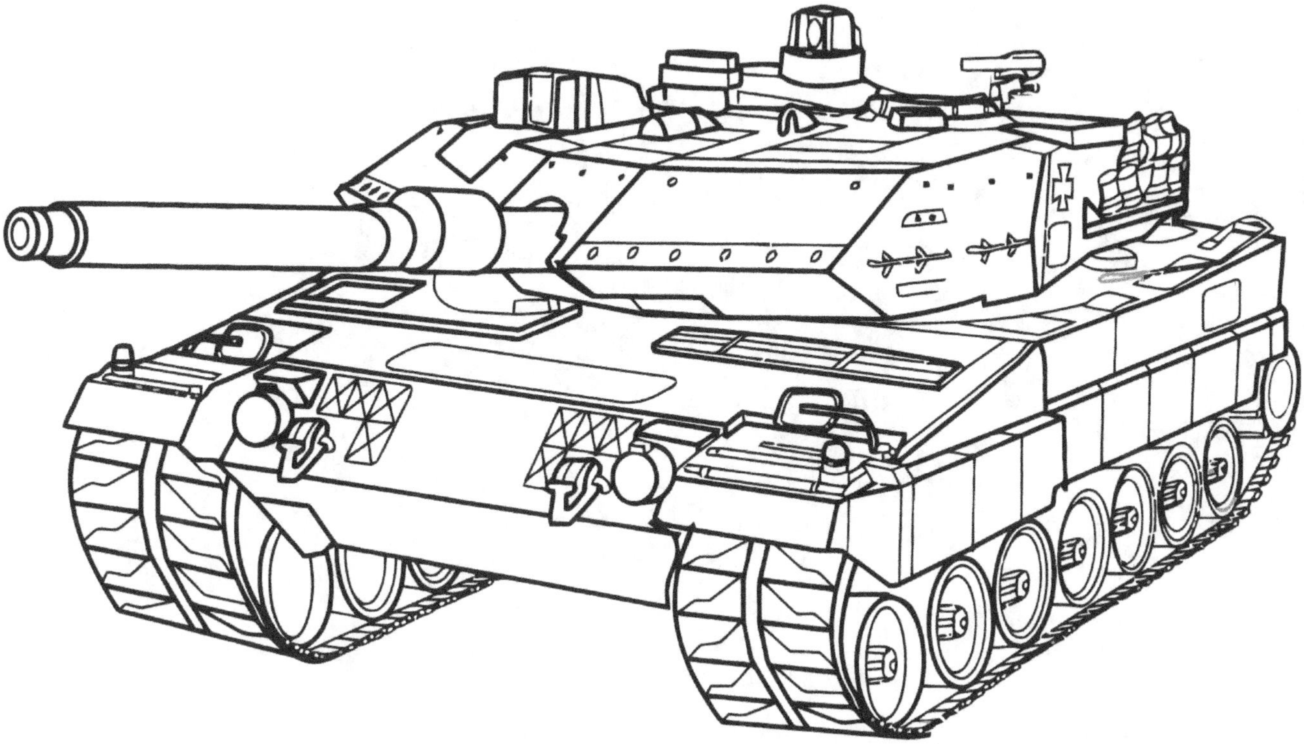

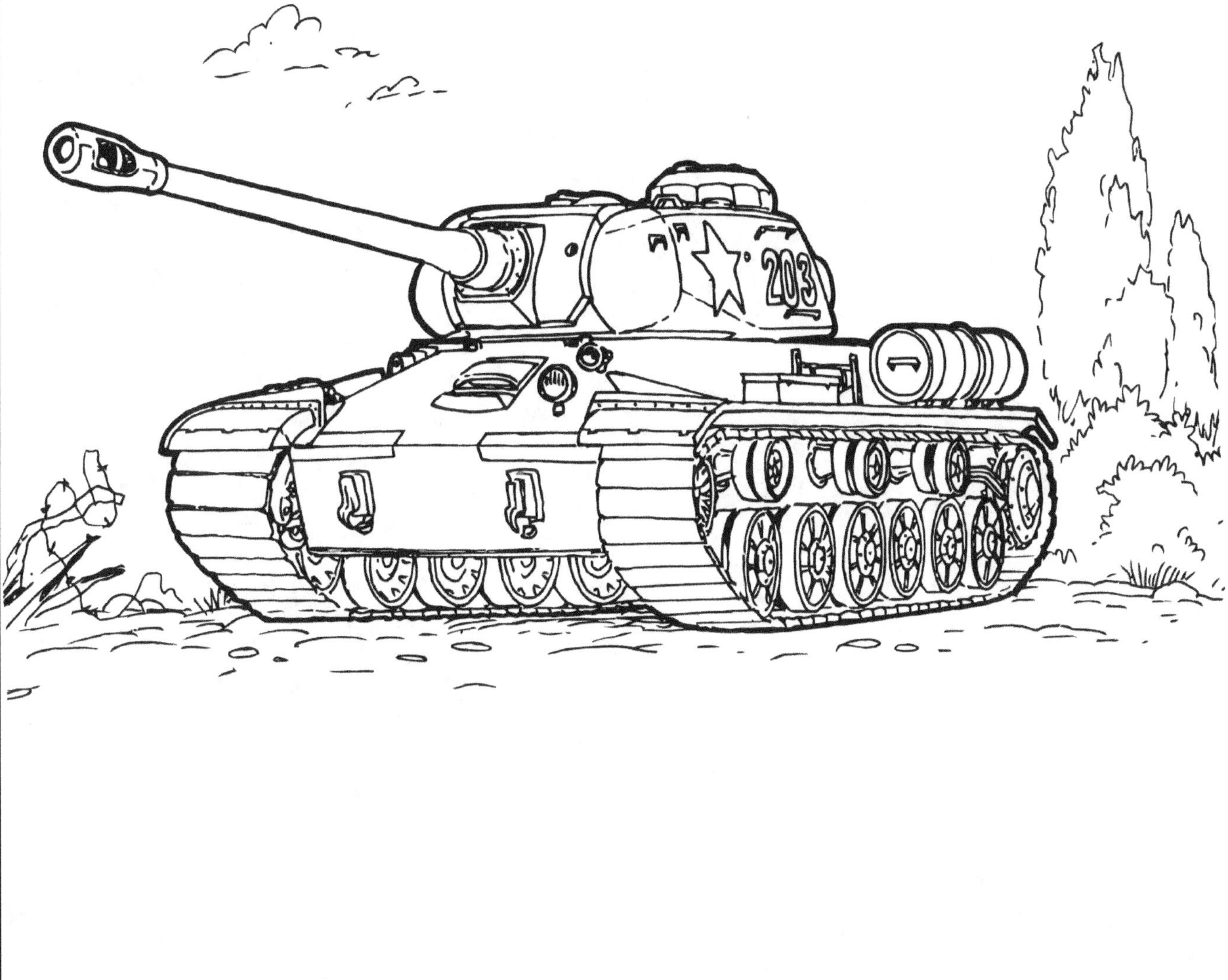
203

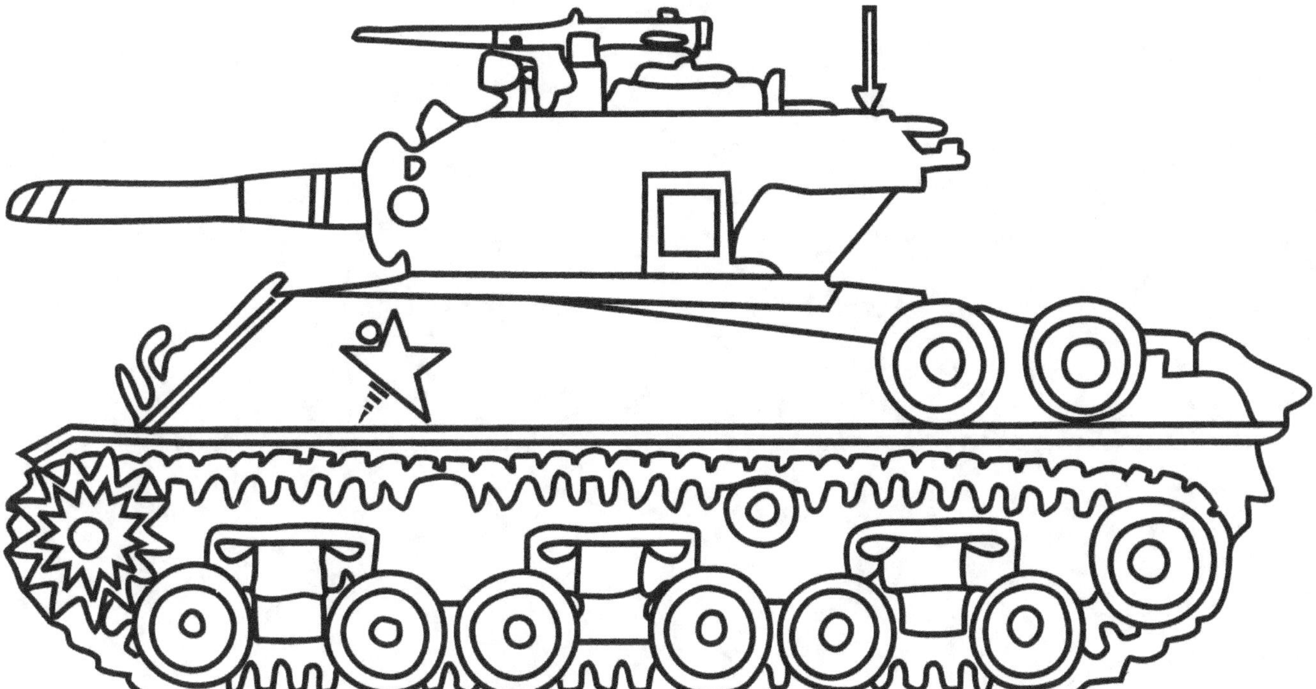

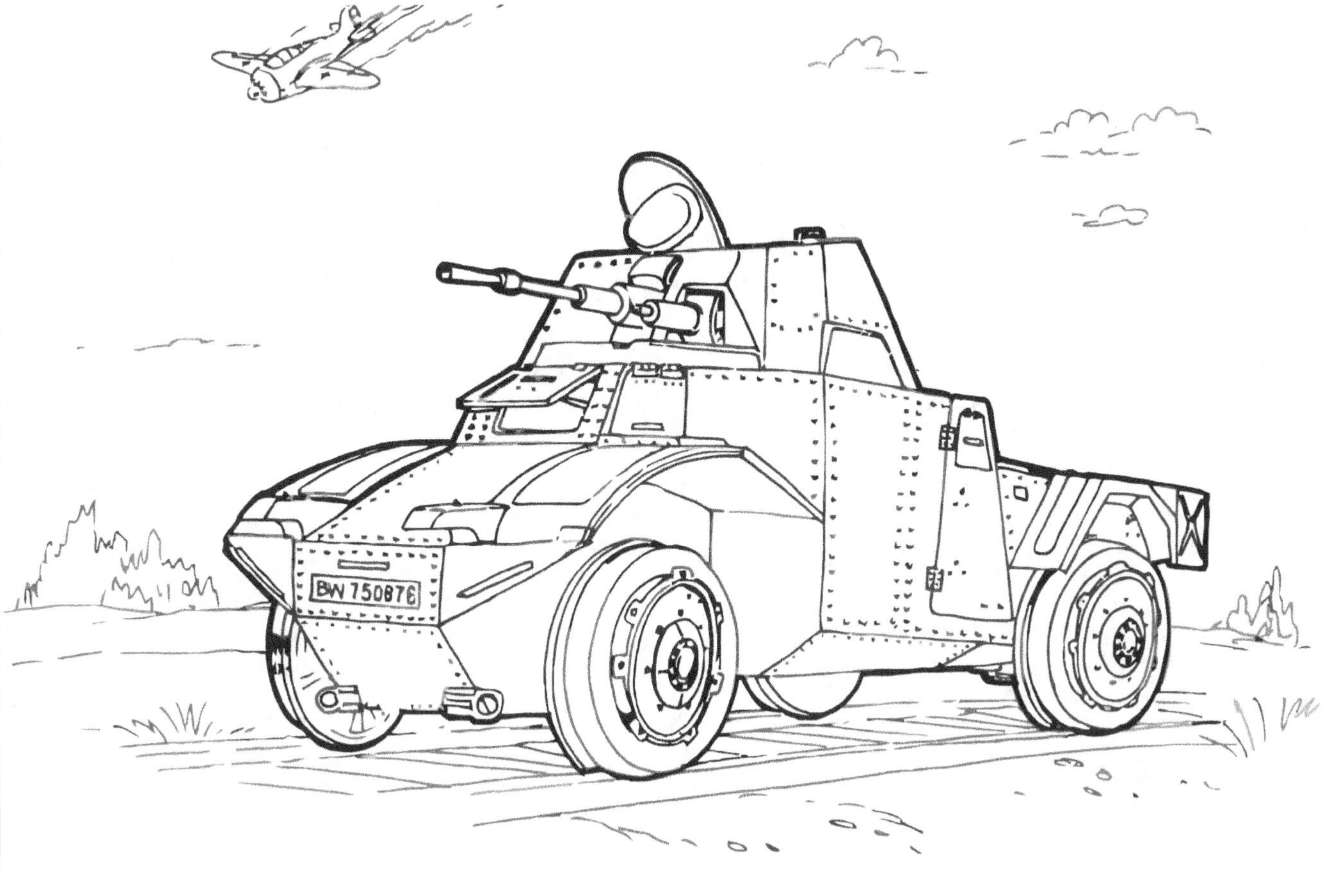
BW 750876

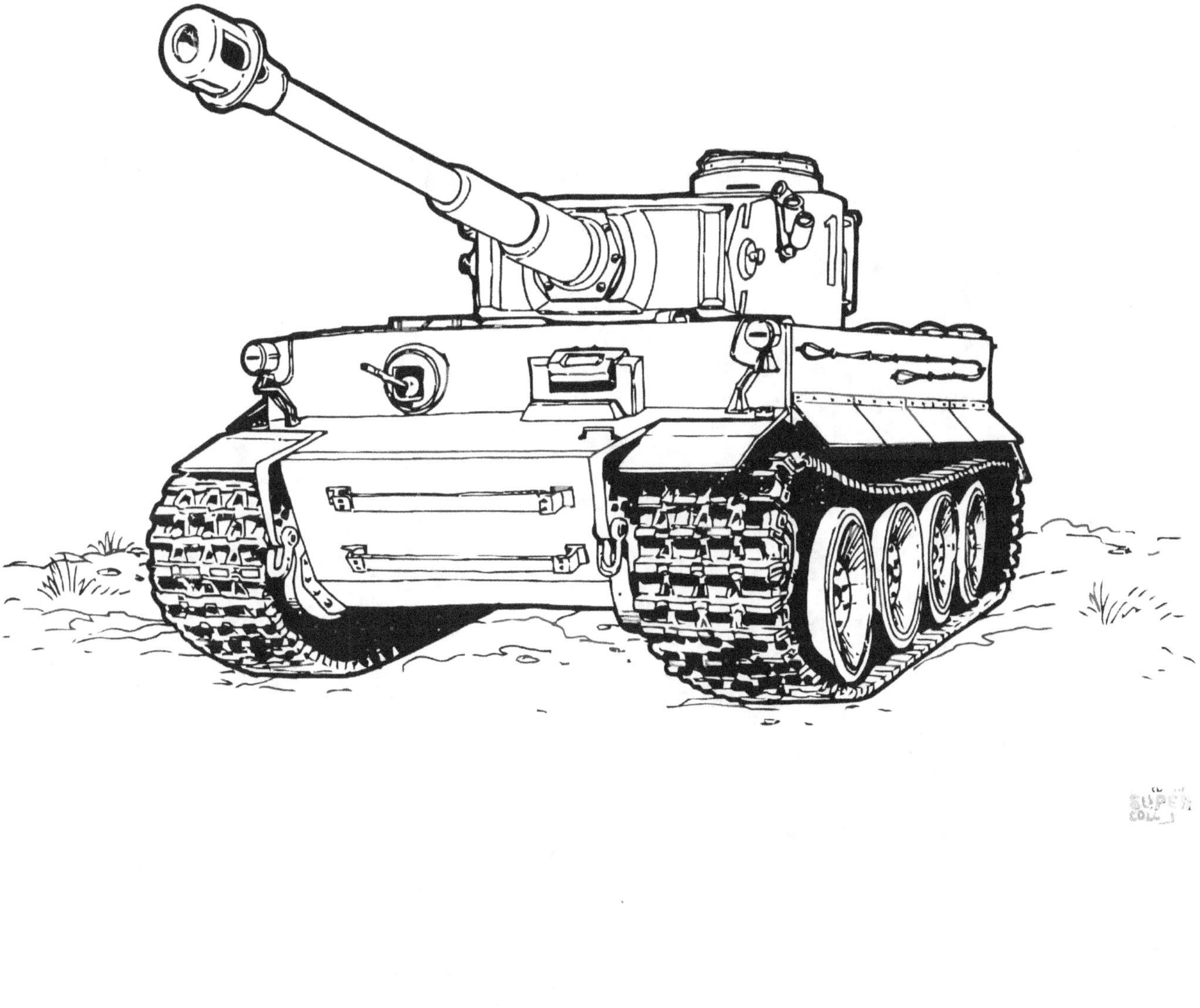

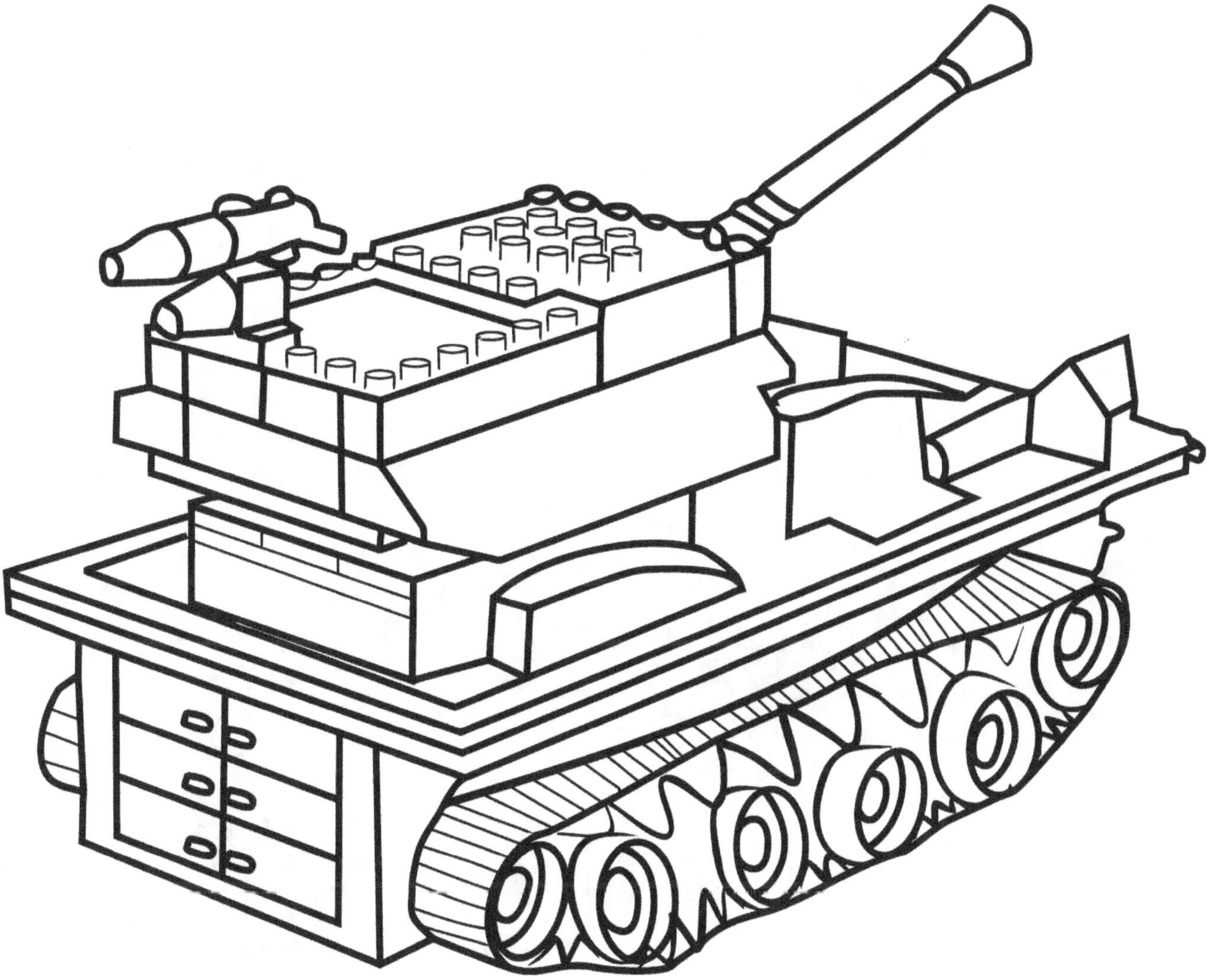

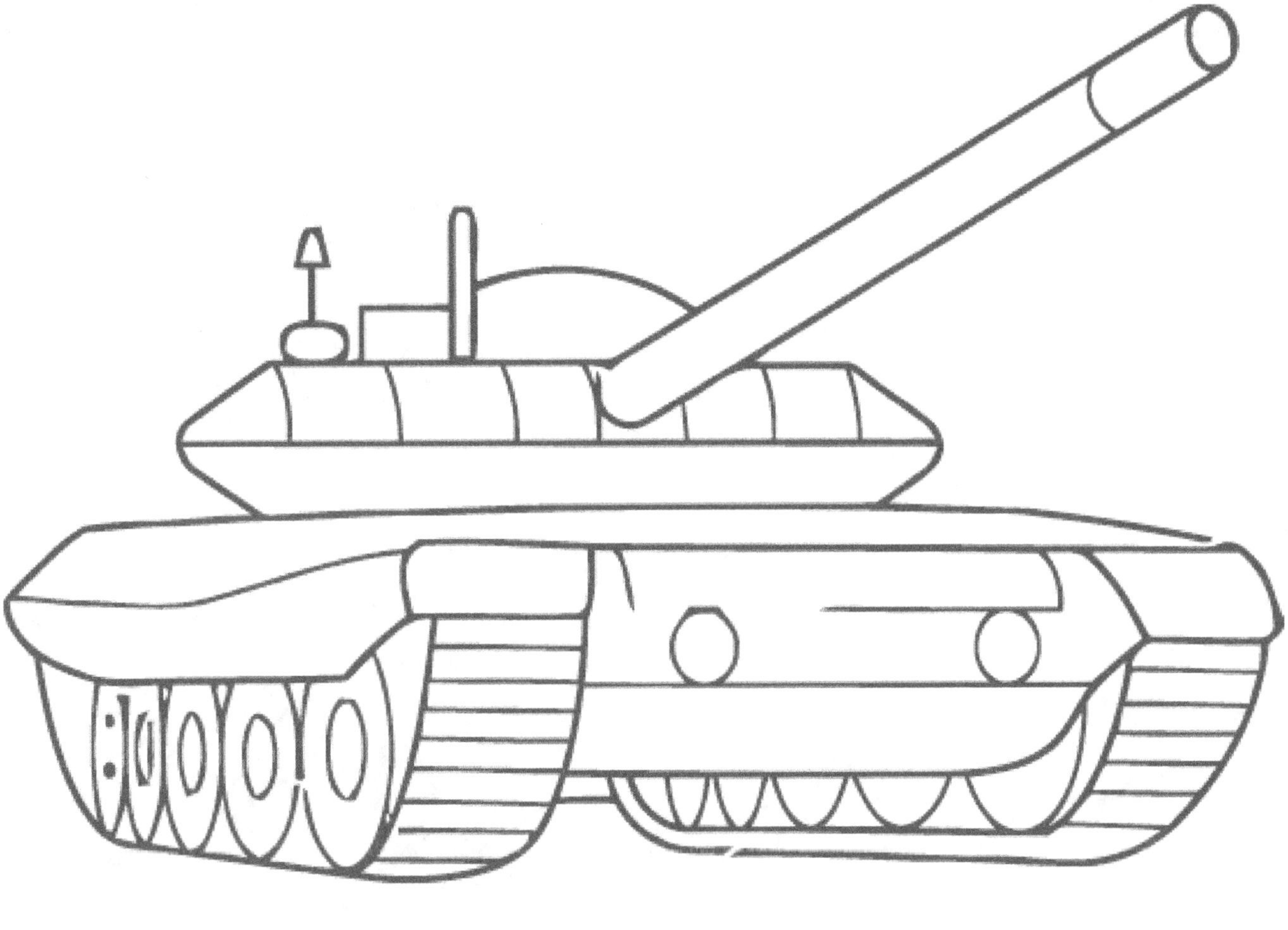

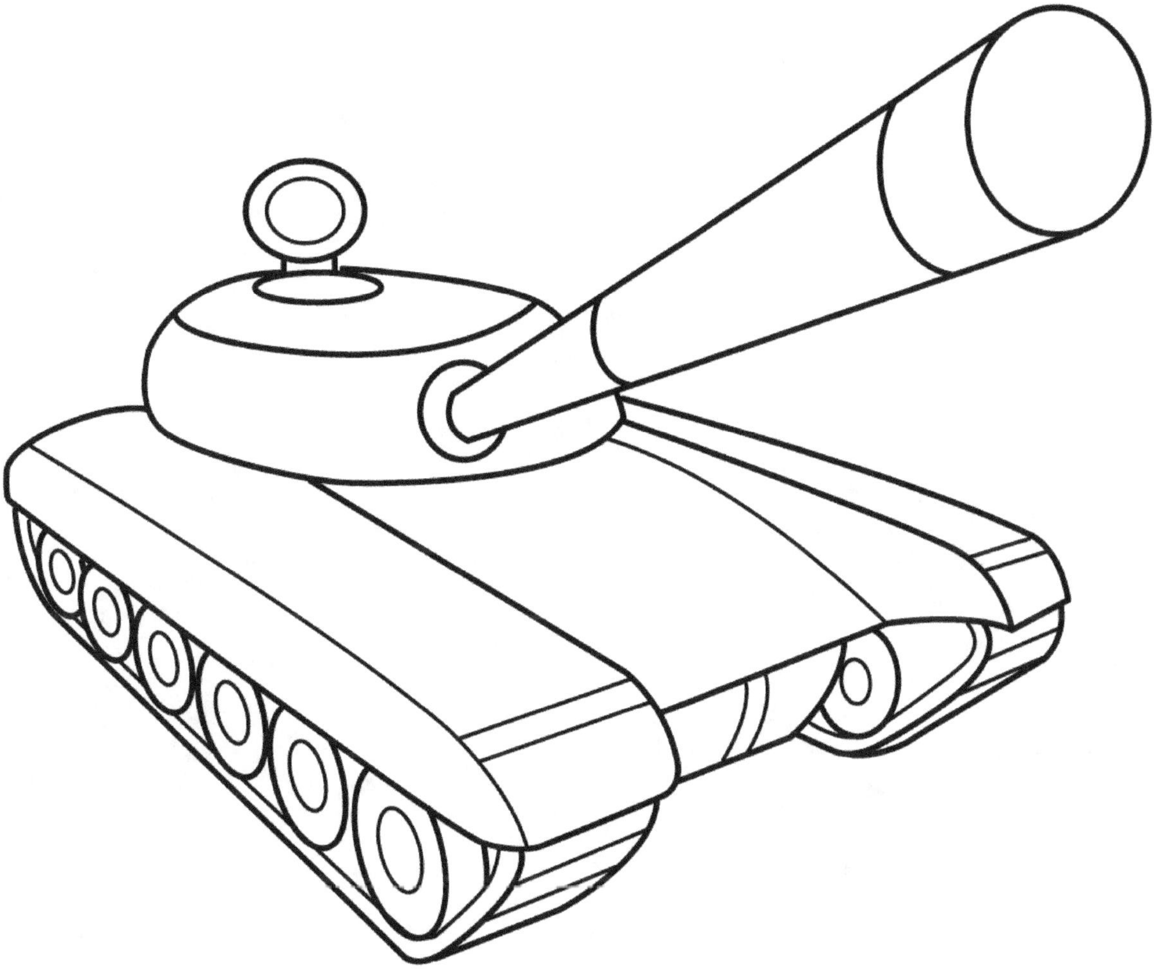

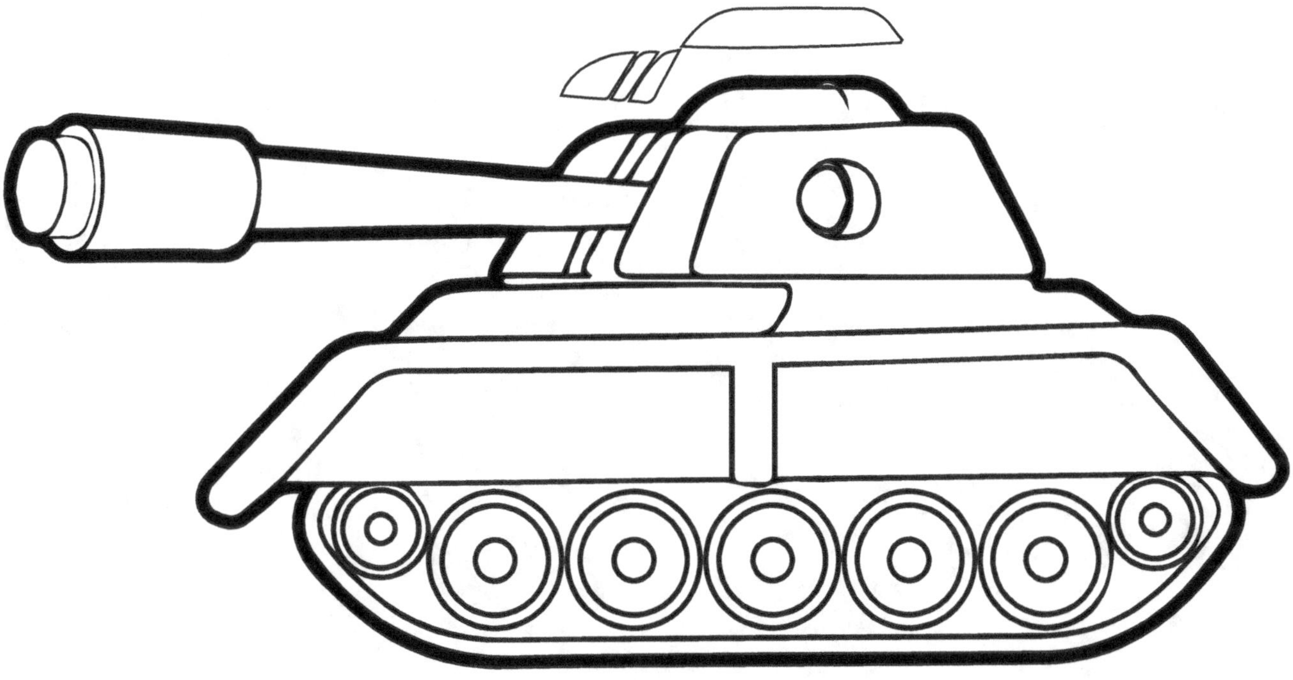

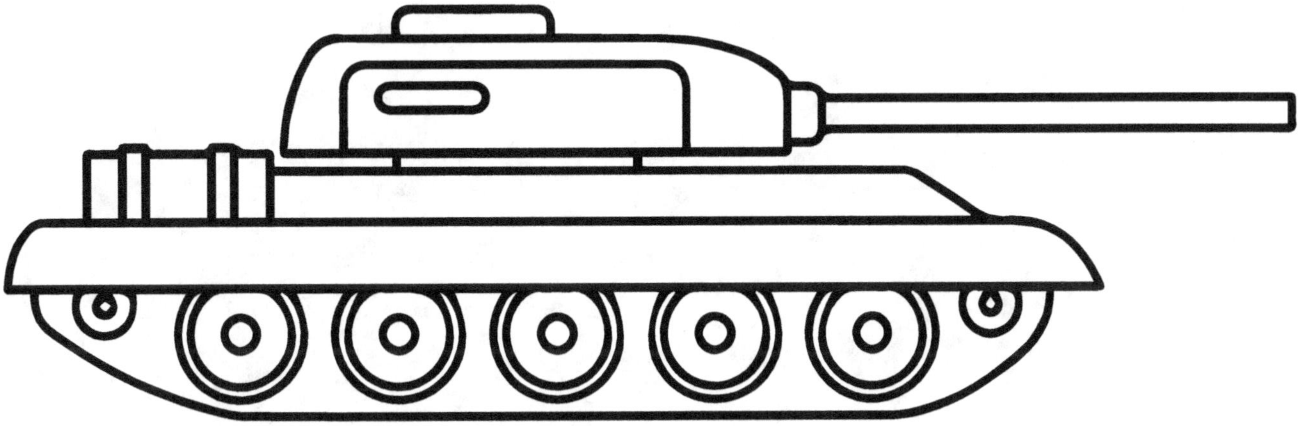

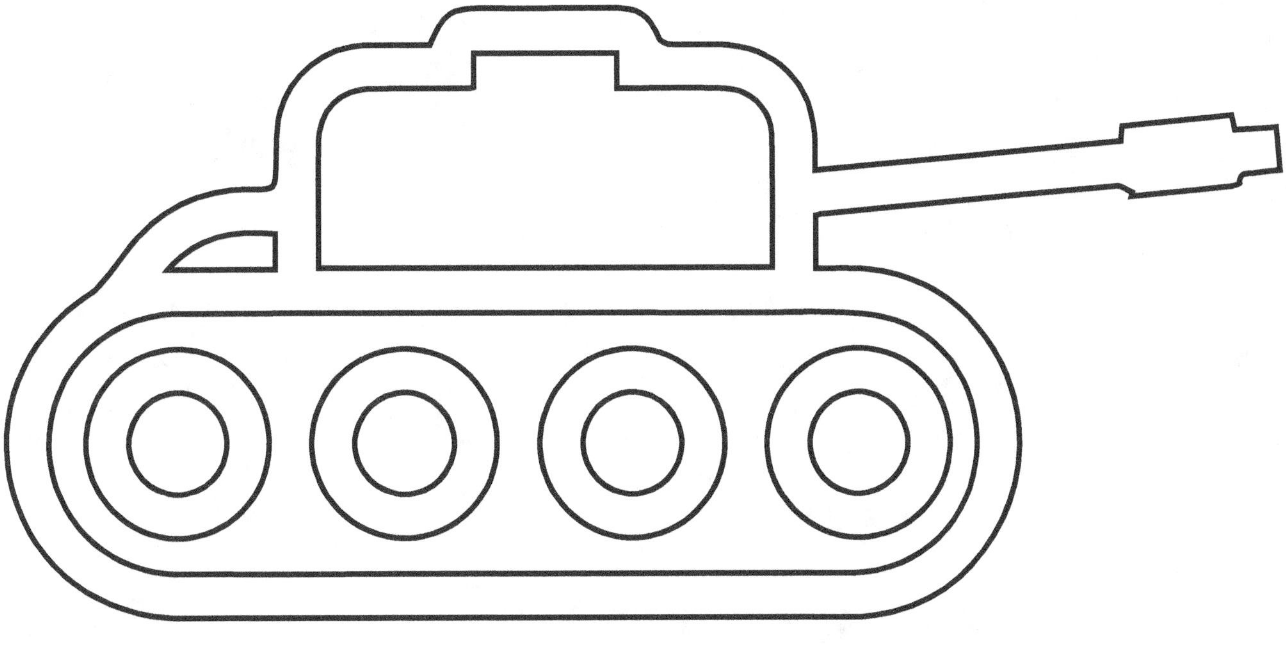

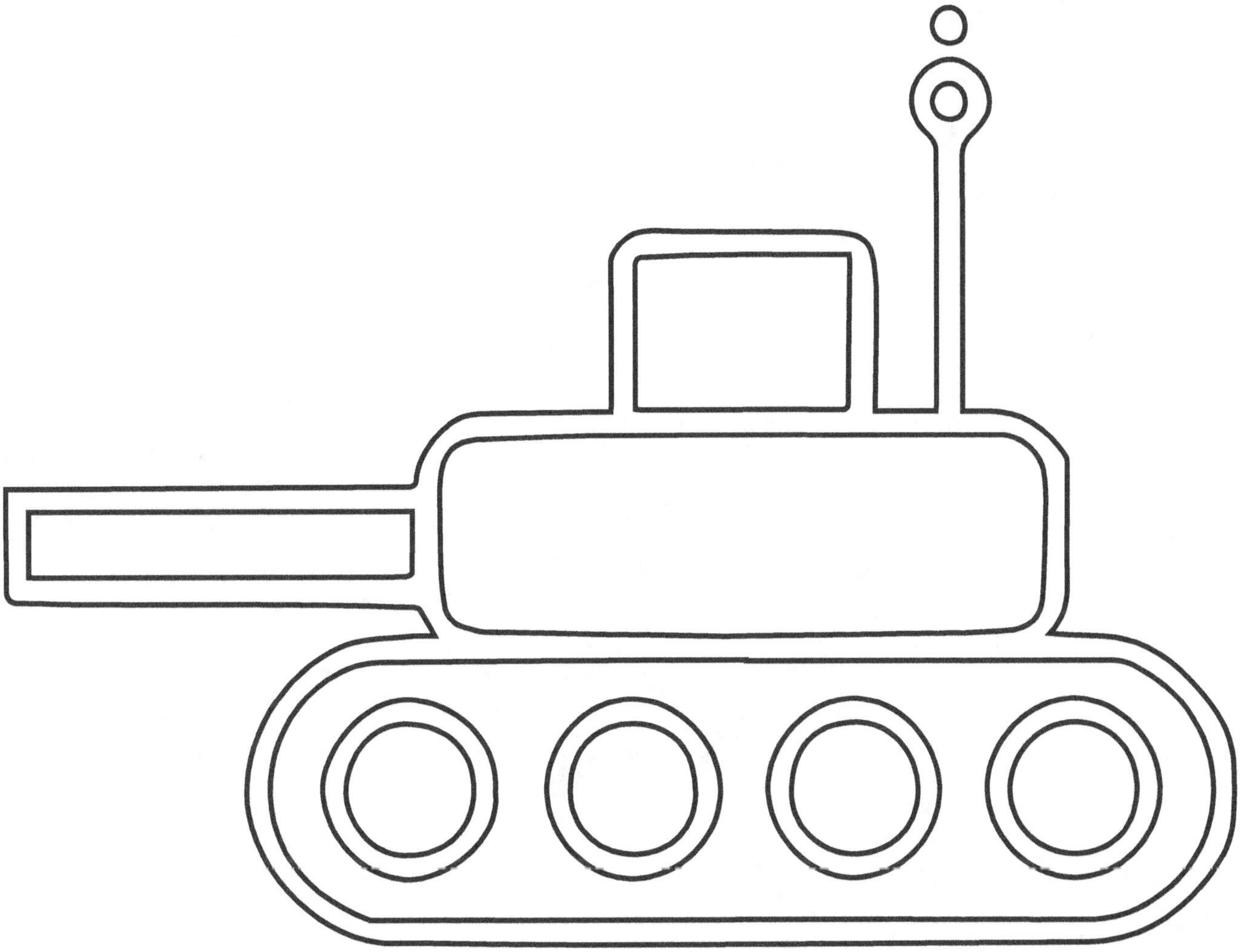

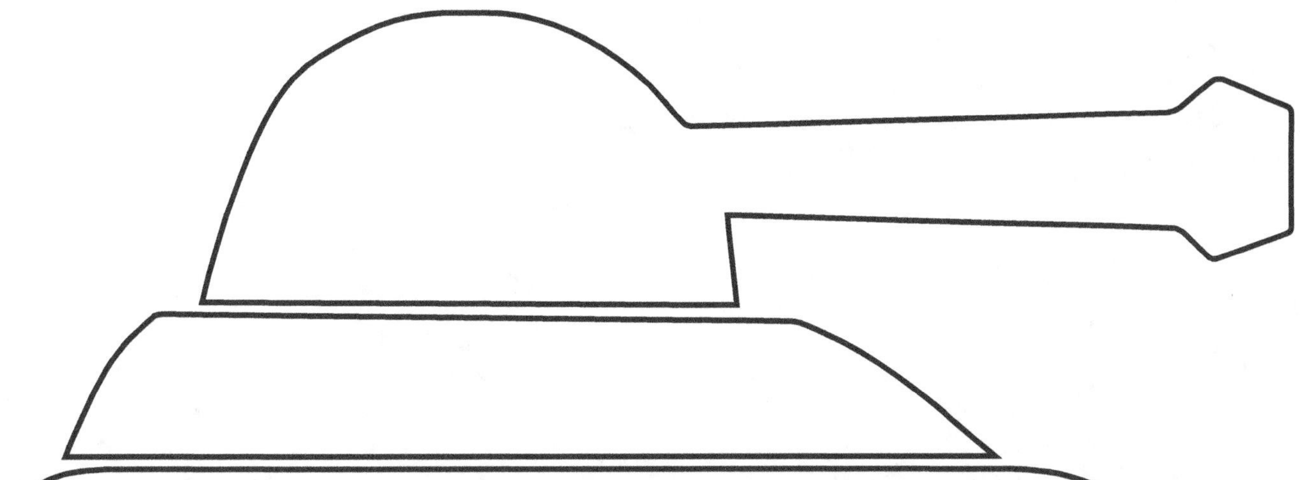

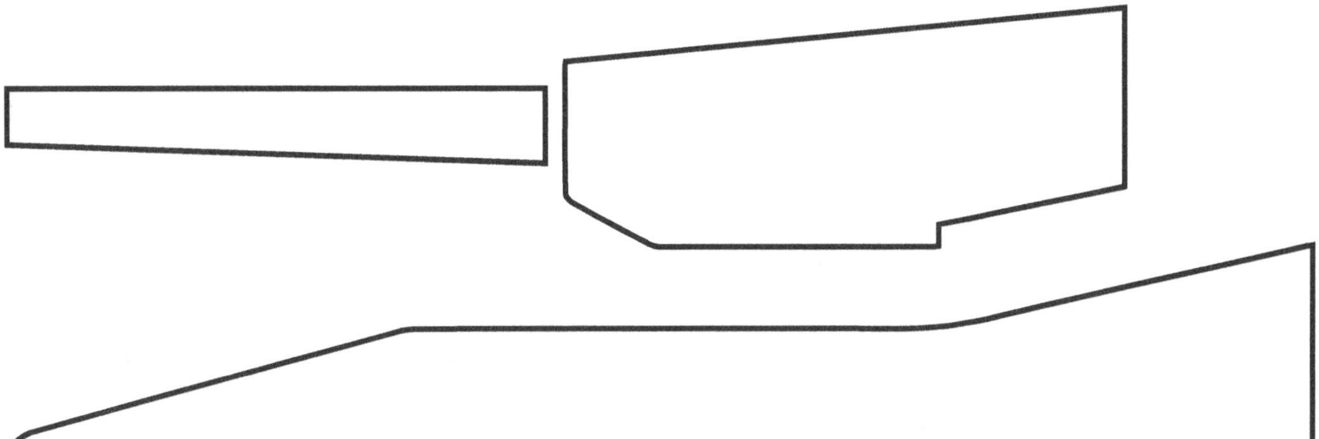

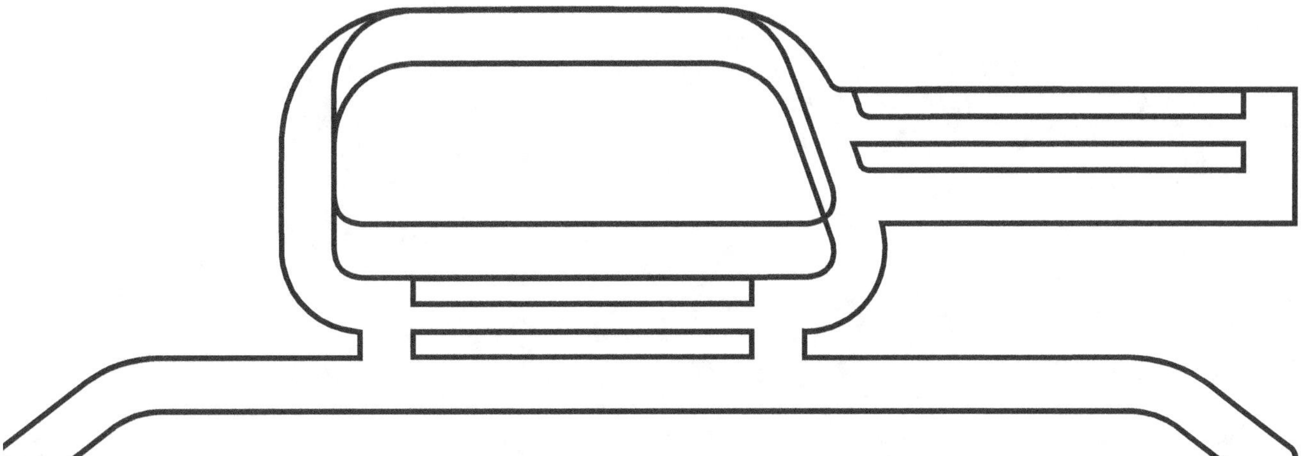

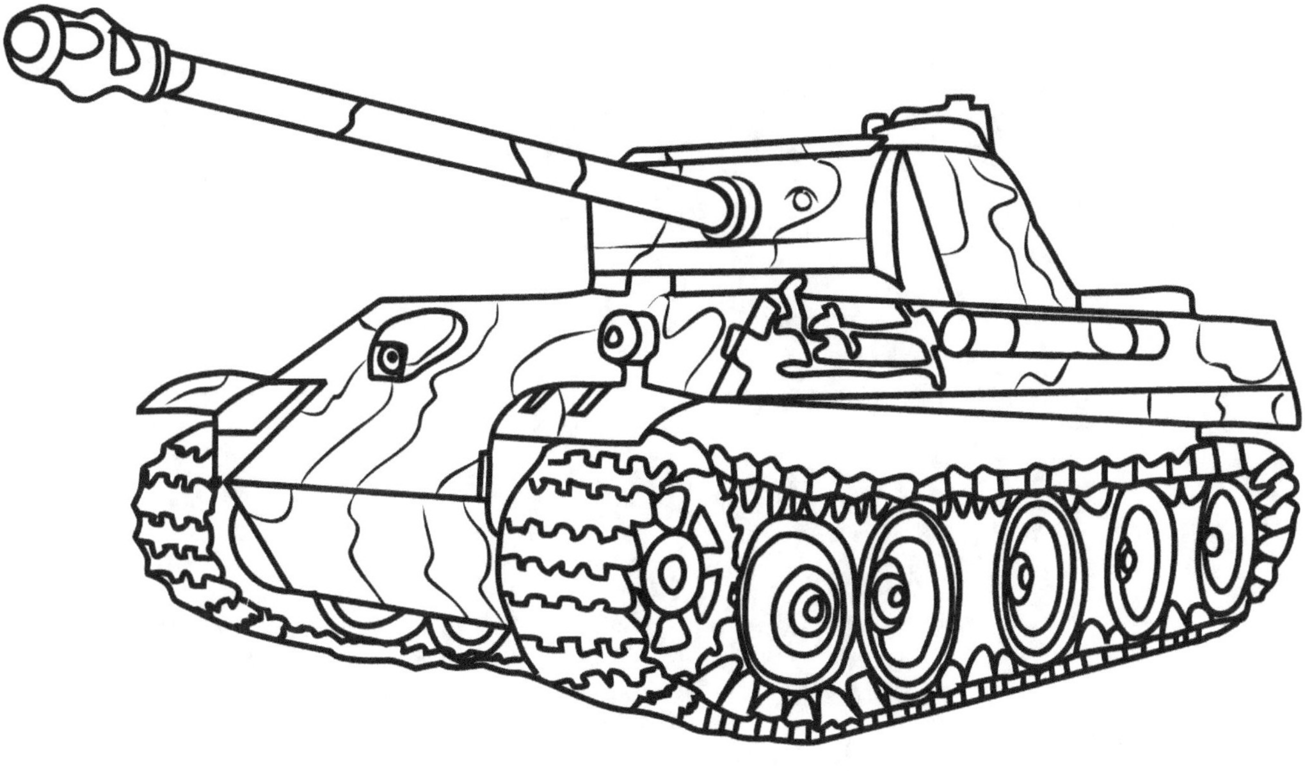

www.ingramcontent.com/pod-product-compliance
Lightning Source LLC
Chambersburg PA
CBHW080512220526
45465CB00006B/2457
* 9 7 9 8 6 6 9 3 8 3 2 5 1 *